Take Courage

A STUDY OF HAGGAI

JENNIFER ROTHSCHILD

Lifeway Press®
Brentwood, Tennessee

ISBN: 979-8-3845-1078-9 • Item: 005849694

Dewey decimal classification: 224.97
Subject headings: DISAPPOINTMENT / BIBLE. O.T. HAGGAI—STUDY AND TEACHING / COURAGE

To order additional copies of this resource, write to Lifeway Resources Customer Service; 200 Powell Place, Suite 100; Brentwood, TN 37027-7707; order online at lifeway.com; fax 615.251.5933; phone toll free 800.458.2772; or email orderentry@lifeway.com.

Printed in the United States of America

Adult Ministry Publishing,
Lifeway Resources,
200 Powell Place, Suite 100,
Brentwood, TN 37027-7707

**EDITORIAL TEAM,
LIFEWAY WOMEN
BIBLE STUDIES**

Becky Loyd
Director,
Lifeway Women

Sarah Doss
Editorial Project
Lead

Mike Wakefield
Content Editor

Mandy Crow
Erin Franklin
Production Editors

Lauren Ervin
Chelsea Waack
Graphic Designers

Contents

ABOUT THE AUTHOR

Take Courage: A Study of Haggai is Jennifer's seventh video-based Bible study with Lifeway. It follows her popular Bible studies, *Psalm 23: The Shepherd With Me, Hosea: Unfailing Love Changes Everything,* and *Me, Myself, and Lies: A Thought-Closet Makeover.*

Jennifer became blind when she was fifteen years old and has experienced firsthand how God gives us courage through His presence, His people, and His Word. Now, more than thirty years later as an author and speaker, she boldly and compassionately teaches women how they can take courage, too.

Known for her substance, signature wit, and down-to-earth style, Jennifer weaves together relatable stories with biblical truths to help women know and live for Christ. She has shared her practical and inspiring messages to audiences across the country and through media outlets including: *The Dr. Phil Show, Good Morning America, Life Today,* and *The Billy Graham Television Special.*

She is the featured teacher and founder of "Fresh Grounded Faith Conferences," host of the *4:13 Podcast,* and publisher of the popular online resource for women in ministry called WomensMinistry.net.

Jennifer and her husband, whom she calls her "very own Dr. Phil," live in Missouri, and have two sons, Connor and Clayton, and a lovely daughter-in-law, Caroline. She's also GiGi to her two grandsons, and that's her favorite name of all!

Besides walking—or being walked by—her little dog Lucy, Jennifer enjoys riding a bicycle built for two with her husband. She is also an avid listener of audiobooks, a C. S. Lewis junkie, and loves dark chocolate and robust coffee—especially when shared with a friend.

Connect with Jennifer at jenniferrothschild.com/takecourage.

INTRODUCTION

Hey, sister!

I'm typing this with a bulky, uncomfortable cast on my left arm. Just as I finished writing this study, I tripped over my open dishwasher door and landed on my wrist. Ouch.

Girl, it's been painful and a pain! Managing the trappings of a broken wrist has been hard but trying to pull myself out of the trap of discouragement I landed in when I fell on my kitchen floor has been even harder.

Healing has been slow. Blindness has made being one-handed even more complicated. And courage, well, it ran out about the time I ran out of my first bottle of Tylenol®!

Discouragement is real. But so is God's presence. And because He is with us, we can take courage—to be who He calls us to be and do what He calls us to do.

That's why I'm so glad you're here! You've got stuff in your life that makes you want to throw in the towel too. It's often the daily drip, drip, drip of defeat or frustration that discourages us. But sister, that's when we can take courage. And our guy, Haggai, will show us how.

So here's how this will go. During the week you'll do daily study. It's OK if you don't finish a day of study or fill in every blank. This is a guilt-free Bible study! Yet, the more you do, the more you'll gain. Then, if you're doing this with a group, you'll gather with your Bible study buddies seven times. You'll pray, watch me teach on video, and discuss what you've discovered in your personal study. Also, if you're the courageous woman leading this group, you'll find helps in the back of this book.

Plus at jenniferrothschild.com/takecourage, you'll find two more things to complement your study. First, I've created a *Haggai* playlist for you to listen to as you do this study. Secondly, you can sign up to get the weekly video teaching summaries. That way, if you missed a word, or a whole video, you can easily catch up.

Sister, I've had you in mind and on my heart as I studied Haggai because I want this to bless you, grow you, and change you just like it has me. So I'm raising my good wrist and cheering you on! Let's take courage together as we take God at His Word.

Love,

Jennifer

Group session 1

Rather than a formal leader guide in the back, we've provided what we hope is a simple and functional group plan on these pages with an additional word to leaders in the back. Each week will begin with a two-page group guide like this. I suggest you divide your group time into three parts: 1. Welcome and prayer; 2. Watch the video; 3. Group discussion of the personal study for the past week and the video you just watched.

The session guide for this first meeting is for us to get to know each other. Then we'll each go do our personal study. (It will be fun, I promise!) Each day, plan to spend a few minutes with that day's study. Don't worry if some days you don't get it all. This isn't a race, and you can come back later. When we meet next group session, we'll have this week's study to discuss. Now let's get to know each other, and I'll join you by way of video.

BEFORE THE VIDEO

Welcome and Prayer

VIDEO NOTES

Haggai 2:4 is an _____ from God—not just an imperative command.

Taking courage comes from taking God at His _____ and trusting His _____.

We need to take the courage that God _____ us so that we can be the women He has _____ us to be and do what He has _____ us to do.

Haggai prophesied at the same time as the prophet _____.[1]

Haggai lived during the same historical period as _____, the Chinese philosopher.[2]

Unfortunately, the Jews did not follow _____ _____.

The Book of Haggai contains four _____ that Haggai preached in four months.

> Would you like to read my written summary of this video teaching? Just go to jenniferrothschild.com/takecourage

The Jews are now under _____ rule.

- King Solomon _____ a temple.
- King Nebuchadnezzar _____ a temple.
- King Cyrus said, "_____ that temple."
- King Jesus said, "I _____ the temple."

Video 1 and Getting to Know Each Other

What is one thing you want this group to know about you?

What drew you to this study of Haggai?

What do you hope to gain from this study?

Your Bible study book comes with access to the videos
that accompany this study. You'll find detailed information
for how to stream the video teaching sessions on the card
inserted in the back of this book. The first video session is
an introduction to the series.

The ABCs of Haggai

Haggai Highlights

598 BC

King Nebuchadnezzar laid siege to Jerusalem and the first deportation of Jews to Babylon took place (2 Kings 24:10-16).

586 BC

Nebuchadnezzar destroyed Jerusalem and the second deportation of Jews to Babylon took place (2 Kings 25:8-21; Jer. 39:8-10; 40:7; 52:12-34).

538 BC

- King Cyrus of Persia defeated the Babylonians.

- First group of Jews, including Zerubbabel and Joshua, returned to Jerusalem and began to rebuild the temple, completing the foundation (Ezra 3:8-11).

- Opposition arose, and the temple rebuilding was stopped (Ezra 4:1-5,24).

520 BC

- Haggai appeared on the scene, urging Jews to get back to work on the temple.

- First day, sixth month (August 29), Haggai's first sermon (Hag. 1–11)

- Twenty-fourth day, sixth month (September 21), temple reconstruction began again (Hag. 1:14-15).

- Twenty-first day, seventh month (October 17), Haggai's second sermon (Hag. 2:1-9)

- Twenty-fourth day, ninth month (December 18), Haggai's third and fourth sermons (Hag. 2:10-23)

515 BC

Temple was finished (Ezra 6:15).

Approximate dates are from *The New American Commentary—Volume 21a, Haggai & Malachi* and from the *Holman Old Testament Commentary.*

Day 1

IT'S SHORT, BUT IT'S NOT SHALLOW

Hey, my friend! I'm so grateful you're choosing to take courage right along with me. You're going to love our guy Haggai! Which, by the way, in case you aren't sure how to pronounce his name—just rhyme it with "guy" like "our guy Haggai," and you're good to go.

If you're not familiar with Haggai, don't worry. Neither was I. One day, while reading the Book of Haggai, I thought, *I feel like those people he's preaching to!* In other words, discouraged. It wasn't full blown throw-in-the-towel kind of discouragement; I was just "weary in well doing," to quote the King James Version (Gal. 6:9). I felt like I had about as much courage as that scaredy-cat lion in the *Wizard of Oz*! Nothing was really wrong; life was good.

But sometimes, real life brings real discouragement, doesn't it? You've felt it. You may be feeling it right now. When the mundane of life piles up, when the happy ending of our story feels a million miles away, when the joy-squashers and courage-killers won't leave us alone, we can find ourselves wanting to quit.

We all need encouragement. Encouragement is oxygen for the discouraged soul. Girl, I had no idea how much encouragement was tucked into Haggai's thirty-eight verses. So, let's do this! You are about to step into one of the shortest books of the Bible but watch your step because short does not mean shallow. The Book of Haggai is deeper than you think!

Turn to the Old Testament Book of Haggai. We are going to read all of it but don't panic. It's only two chapters long!

Before you read Haggai, review the following questions. Then, as you read, jot down some notes:

What phrases do I read more than once?

> ### GO DEEPER
>
> Check out page 182 in the back of the book to find a list of resources for studying the Bible, including some of my online favorites.

What emotions do I experience?

What passages are confusing?

What seems challenging in the book?

What words or verses sound hopeful?

Take a minute and review what you wrote. Pause and pray over each area where you jotted notes. Ask God to give you clarity over the next few weeks about what confuses you. Ask Him for courage to face what challenges you. Thank God for the hope you found and praise Him for the ways His faithfulness is reflected in these verses.

Once you've said "Amen," let's start at the beginning again. Literally. I'm pausing to pour my coffee now, so pause and pour yourself some, too! Or, of course, tea, Coke®, or whatever you like will be just fine with Haggai and me.

Look at Haggai 1:1 and jot down the name of the author.

I know, it's obvious, but what is obvious is often overlooked. Let's pause for a minute to see what is hidden in the author's name. Look in your favorite online Bible resource and find the meaning behind Haggai's name. (Hint: You can just Google "Hebrew meaning of Haggai.")

What does Haggai's name mean?

It seems everyone agrees that Haggai's name means "festive" or "festival"—but they don't all agree on the reason. Some scholars believe it's because Haggai was born on a feast day, so he was named accordingly. Kind of like if you were born on a warm July day, and your mama named you Summer. But others believe that "festive" points to the joyous nature of Haggai's prediction; his prophecy is encouraging![3]

Since the Book of Haggai only has two chapters, go back and read it once more. This time through, record the joyous predictions and/or encouraging promises you find in the reference listed below.

PROMISE	REFERENCE
	Haggai 1:13; 2:4
	Haggai 2:5
	Haggai 2:7
	Haggai 2:8
	Haggai 2:9
	Haggai 2:22
	Haggai 2:23

God promised His presence and His Spirit would be among His people. He promised He would shake the nations, and the latter glory would be greater than the former. He promised He would fill His house with glory, and He would make Zerubbabel like His signet ring. (If that one makes no sense right now, don't worry; it will.) Finally, God also promised His peace. Worth partying over, right?

 I'm sharing my personal *Haggai* playlist with you! As you're getting to know Haggai this week, listen to the Session One songs of my *Haggai* playlist at **jenniferrothschild.com/takecourage**.

Those predictions and promises were encouraging to the people of Haggai's day. And you'll soon discover how encouraging they will be to you, too. In fact, my prayer is that you will find courage and encouragement as you study these verses along with me.

Well, my mug is empty, so we'll pick this up tomorrow. I'm praying for you and cheering you on. See you tomorrow!

OUR GUY HAGGAI

On Day One, we started with the basics of Haggai. Let's continue that simple approach and look at the ABCs of Haggai over the next three days. We'll start with *A*, the author.

If Haggai had a profile on LinkedIn®, it might look something like this:

- I was born in Judah before 586 BC.[4]
- I'm the only person in the Old Testament with the name Haggai.[5]
- I began prophetic ministry in Jerusalem in 520 BC.[6]
- I'm the first of the prophets to minister to Israel following her return from Babylonian captivity.
- I successfully exhorted the people to complete the task of rebuilding the temple.

Nice profile, huh?

Haggai was a man whom God raised up at a specific time for a specific mission. Some scholars believe he was older when called to serve.[7] If this is true, try picturing Haggai in a contemporary setting: a card-carrying AARP-er, drinking his discount coffee from McDonald's®. I love that! It reminds me that no matter how young or old we are, we can also be raised up for a specific time and a specific mission.

You can embrace any season of life with purpose! Learn how on my podcast. Go to **413podcast.com/22** to listen.

> How does the way you feel about your age impact how you view your purpose or usefulness?

Sometimes, when we're young, we get discouraged because we feel we need a ton more experience before we are usable. On the other hand, when we're in the sunset years, we can get downright down because we feel our usefulness has diminished right along with our energy (or natural hair color).

Pause here for a second and find the following verses of Scripture. Jot down what they suggest about your age and usefulness.

Isaiah 46:4 even to your old age, I am He, & even to your gray hairs I will carry you.

Psalm 71:18 when I'm old, don't forsake me, My God, till I declare your power to the next generation.

Psalm 92:12-15 They will still bear fruit in old age, they'll stay fresh & green proclaiming "the Lord is upright, He is my Rock"

Acts 2:17 Last Days: Daughters will prophesy, sons will visions & old men will dream.

1 Timothy 4:12 Let no one despise you for your youth. be an example. in speech, conduct, love faith & purity.

I'd love to hear your personal mission! Share it on Twitter® or Instagram® and be sure to tag me (@JennRothschild) and use the #TakeCourageStudy hashtag.

These verses show us that no matter how young or old you may be, you are in the game, sister! You may be at the starting line, somewhere on the sidelines trying to catch your breath, or close to the finish line, but you are still in it to win it! You are part of what God is doing and wants to do in our world. Be encouraged that you are never too young or too old for kingdom work. In Christ, there are no has-beens and no wannabes!

As you study the Book of Haggai, ask God to make you aware of why He has raised you up for this specific time and how He wants to use you.

Do you know your current mission assignment? Take a moment to think and pray about this. Jot down what God may have raised you up for. Write out what you think your personal mission is for this season of your life. (Remember, there are no small missions!)

raise Jase
Teacher?

You can relate to Haggai in lots of ways.

Think about it. Every season of life represents the end of an era and the start of something new. Perhaps young Haggai had been in a season of captivity in Babylon. Old Haggai went back home and had to start all over again in a brand-new season. When we're younger, we may be at the end of a bad relationship or at the beginning of a new career. When we're older, we may be stuck in a season of compromised health or finding our way with an empty nest. In between those seasons, we may just be coming out of a difficult divorce or moving to a new city.

Like Haggai, we all have seasons when we feel stuck, held captive, or longing to be free. We all also face seasons of new beginnings that often hold more questions than answers. Where are you in that cycle?

I've been held captive by . . .

I've had to start all over again or want to start all over again when it comes to . . .

I'm in a new season of . . .

Sister, you can relate to Haggai, right? Some scholars think he may have been one of the exiles in Babylon.[8] If that's the case, he would have had to navigate that transition from slavery to freedom, old patterns to new beginnings, familiar bondage to uncertain optimism.

And you and I have the same opportunities, don't we? I hope you're starting to see yourself in this little Book of Haggai. Your life can be found in his story, too. We'll get to know Haggai (and ourselves) a lot better as we move through this study, but that's enough for today.

Oh wait! I should pause with a major P.S. here. The human author of Haggai is our friend Haggai, but the ultimate author of the Book of Haggai is God Himself (2 Tim. 3:16-17). I figured you knew that, but, girl, I didn't want that foundational, life-changing, history-altering fact to slip past you. That means that God's Word, including the Book of Haggai, is alive and God-breathed. In turn, it can give you life and breathe life into your story. OK?

OK! Tomorrow, we are moving to the letter *B*. See you then!

Day 3

THE BACKSTORY AND YOUR STORY

Well, hey there! So glad you're working through all the ABCs of Haggai with me. Getting familiar with these facts and context will help your heart grasp the deep message as we move through all thirty-eight verses.

Today, we're covering the *B*, the backstory. Let's turn the biblical calendar back a few decades to see what the Jews experienced so we can better understand how they must have felt. It all started in 2 Kings 25. Go there and answer the following questions:

Who attacked whom (vv.1-2)? **Babylon attacked Jerusalem**

List some of the awful things the Jews endured because of Babylon's attack (vv. 3-16 or 2 Chron. 36:17-20).

famine

Awful, isn't it? In 586 BC, King Nebuchadnezzar left Jerusalem a wasteland—the people starving, the temple destroyed, the walls torn down, and all the houses burned.[9] Most of the Jews were taken captive. Only a remnant of poor people was left behind to farm the land (2 Kings 25:12). Simply put, it was devastating.

Before we move on, I want us to walk a few steps in the Jews' shoes and imagine the state of their hearts. How do you think they must have felt?

List a few adjectives below that describe the emotions the Jews may have experienced.

Hopeless. Afraid. Discouraged. Dejected. Forgotten. Despondent.

Those words describe how I think I would feel if I had been in the Jews' place.

GO DEEPER

Why Psalm 137? Some believe that this psalm was penned by Jeremiah when the people of God were captives in Babylon, likely toward the latter end of their captivity.[10]

Read Psalm 137 to get a glimpse of their experience.

They wept. They longed for home. I can just see them by the river, heads hung low, demoralized, and despondent.

Have you ever felt that discouraged? If so, name the time and the reason.

If you can't think of an exact time, what kinds of experiences bring out those feelings of discouragement for you?

My experience hit me hard several years ago and showed up out of the blue. Girl, my maiden name is Jolly, and it fits me—I've got the happy going on! But when blindness met menopause, they didn't play nice. The result was depression. I'd love to say it was a onetime event that I no longer deal with. But sometimes it creeps back in when I least expect it. It is so discouraging.

Most of us have stories similar to the Jews' backstory—times when our hopes were exiled, our relationships were laid to waste, and discouragement and disappointment lay like rubble around us. Maybe you're in one of those seasons now. Just remember: God promises us hope, just like He did for the Jews.

But perhaps hope doesn't look like we expect it to. Hmmm . . .

Hope for the Jews came in the form of another conquering king. Fast forward a few decades, when Babylon got a bitter taste of her own medicine. Cyrus of Persia was now in charge.

Read 2 Chronicles 36:22-23.

What did Cyrus do for the Jews with his newfound power?

Yes! The Jews were allowed to go home. They could finally leave the captivity of Babylon. About fifty thousand Jews returned. And perhaps our buddy Haggai was one of them.

> I bet they showed up fired up! That's usually how we feel with a new beginning, right? So the Jews went home and got busy rebuilding the temple. But then . . . read Ezra 4:24 and jot down what happened next.

After the Jews got home, the same people who had run for their hammers and nails to rebuild the temple ran out of steam and stopped their rebuilding project.

And, with that my dear, we are caught up with the backstory. As we study this book, we'll get an understanding of why the Jews quit rebuilding. Believe me, we can learn a lot from them.

But think about this before we move on: in captivity, the Jews felt discouragement, right? And rightly so. I can't think of a situation much more discouraging than being dragged from your homeland and being stuck in a foreign land. But when the Jews returned home and started to rebuild, they became discouraged and quit.

> What does that fact teach you about the source of discouragement?

We often assume that when all is going well—when we are free and moving forward— there should be no discouragement. But, sister, discouragement ultimately never comes from an outside source; discouragement is an inside job!

Sure, many discouraging situations are filled with joy-killers, hope-squashers, and naysayers. (We'll meet some of them from Haggai's day next week.) But discouragement rises from within us. We can learn from Haggai how to take courage no matter where we find ourselves. Even when everything around us is discouraging, we can remain encouraged and motivated.

As you finish up today's study, think about that place or thing in your life that you feel most discouraged about. Just linger here with your Father God and be honest with Him.

> Where in your life do you fight defeat? Record it here with a prayer of faith asking God to give you courage and teach you how you can apply the lessons of Haggai to your discouragement.

> Dear God,

> Amen.

 Girl, I promise you that grace and glory are in your story no matter what discouragement or defeat you feel or face.

How God called you to Him, the pits you've fallen in, the small victories and the big blunders, the junk from your past that He's forgiven—all that is your backstory, your testimony. God can use it—and you—to encourage someone. Don't be ashamed of your story. You never know who needs to take courage, and you may be the one who gives it!

God's got us, and I'm so glad you're hanging out with me and our new friend, Haggai. See you tomorrow!

Z AND THE BIG THREE

It's a sunny day here, and I just poured my coffee. I'm drinking from a mug emblazoned with the words: *She believed she could so she did.* That nifty little phrase inspired my prayer for you today as you study. I prayed you would believe God can accomplish in you what feels bigger than you. I pray that as you read God's Word today, you feel His presence.

Pause and ask Him to be your Teacher as we get to know the characters in Haggai. May God use them to help us know ourselves. Amen!

Remember where we left off yesterday? We sped through the background of the Babylonian captivity, and now the Jews are home. They started rebuilding the temple, but somewhere along the way, they got discouraged and stopped. Haggai stepped into the story here. God called him to speak correction and encouragement to the discouraged and distracted Jews. But he wasn't in it alone.

Today, let's look at C, other characters in Haggai I want you to meet.

Turn to Ezra 3:2.

Write down the names in the verse:

Yep, Zerubbabel and Joshua (called "Jeshua" in Ezra) partnered with Haggai in the rebuilding process. Haggai wasn't alone, and you aren't alone either, sister. Many of us are characters playing a part in your story, too.

Tomorrow, we'll get to know Joshua. Today, let's settle in with Zerubbabel. First of all, why is his name so hard to say and spell?! Can we just call him Z, please?

Z is an important part of the Book of Haggai and the bigger gospel story. Let's find out who he was—even if we can hardly spell or pronounce his name!

Do a word search in the Old Testament for Zerubbabel's name. Then, based on the verses you find, describe who he was—most importantly, who he was to the Jews—and what he did. I found a few to start with.

1 Chronicles 3:17-19 • Nehemiah 7:5-7 • Haggai 1:1; 2:21 • Matthew 1:12

Zerubbabel was . . .

Zerubbabel's role was . . .

Zerubbabel was the governor of Judah, put in charge by King Darius. His main job was to oversee the rebuilding of the temple and the restoration of the temple services. Let's discover three amazingly significant things about him that set him apart and put Zerubbabel smack dab in the middle of the gospel story, our story.

1. Zerubbabel the Son

Review 1 Chronicles 3:17-19 and Matthew 1:12.

What can you deduce from these verses about Zerubbabel, his family, and his lineage?

Zerubbabel was a descendant of Shealtiel and the grandson of Judah's King Jehoiachin. If you climb all the branches of that family tree, you'll discover that means he was a descendant of David; he was of royal blood. Zerubbabel was not only in the Davidic line, but he also reestablished the Davidic throne.

That's a big deal because God promised David his family would always be on the throne.

Read Isaiah 11:1-5,10 and Revelation 22:16.

Based on those verses, who is also in the line of David?

Jesus, our Messiah, is in the lineage of David. That means Z was in the line of Jesus.

2. Zerubbabel the Servant

Read Haggai 2:20-23.

In these verses, Zerubbabel is also called "my servant." This title was often a Messianic reference in the Old Testament.

Check out the following passages of Scripture to see what I mean.

2 Samuel 3:18

1 Kings 11:34

Isaiah 42:1-9

Ezekiel 34:23

How is the phrase *servant* compatible with *Messiah*?

> ### ZERUBBABEL'S DAD
>
> In 1 Chronicles 3:17-19 Zerubbabel's father is listed as Pedaiah, the brother of Shealtiel. Apparently Salathiel (AKA Shealtiel, the same guy) died without a son, and his brother Pedaiah married Shealtiel's widow who gave birth to Zerubbabel. The purpose of such a marriage was to maintain the dead husband's line, so that means Zerubbabel was legally Salathiel's (Shealtiel's) son— even though, technically to us, he was Shealtiel's nephew. Whew! Now you know![12]

The Messiah was not only expected to be a conquering king, but the prophets made it pretty clear He would also be a servant—a Suffering Servant.

Can you think of any New Testament examples of how Jesus fulfilled this prediction? If you're not sure, read John 13 and Philippians 2.

Jesus washed feet; He served; He was not waited on. Z was a servant, too. He served the people in newly established Jerusalem.

OK, hold that thought and consider number three.

3. Zerubbabel the Signet Ring

Read Haggai 2:23.

How was Zerubbabel described in this verse?

Son? Check. Servant? Check. Those two we have heard before. But signet ring? Hmmm . . . Let's learn about the significance of a signet ring.

Use your favorite search engine or Bible website to find the word *signet* in the Old Testament. Take some notes on people who wore signet rings or places signet rings were used. Then determine what a signet ring represented. I've included what I call "Scripture Starters" to help you get started.

Scripture Starters
Genesis 41:41-43 • 1 Kings 21:8 • Esther 8:8 • Daniel 6:17

Signet rings affirmed authority, honor, or ownership. Every signet ring had an emblem that was unique to the king who wore it. A dollop of soft wax was dripped on the seal of an official document and then impressed with the king's signet, which was usually kept on a ring on his finger. A signet was sort of like the seal of a notary public; it certified the document was genuine.

Read Jeremiah 22:24.

Describe how God pictured King Jehoiachin (Coniah):

When King Jehoiachin was deported to Babylon along with the Jews, he lost his throne. God described it like a signet ring being removed from His own finger.

Now, in Haggai 2:23, God called Zerubbabel the signet ring on His finger, but this time the ring wouldn't be removed. As God's signet ring, Zerubbabel was given a place of honor and authority. As a son in the line of David, God was reinstating the Davidic line. As God's servant, God was dropping a clue through Zerubbabel, giving a nod to the coming Messiah, Jesus Christ.

Zerubbabel was clearly a man chosen by God for a purpose—son, servant, and signet ring is like a trifecta! The big three description isn't given to anyone else in Scripture. What an honor and encouragement for Zerubbabel! They show how significant Zerubbabel was in the rebuilding process, and his presence made it clear God was not absent. Even though the temple wasn't complete, God's plan was still working. Zerubbabel was a reminder that God was in control. His presence was encouraging.

But as significant as Z was, he pointed to the One who would be the ultimate Son, Servant, and Signet Ring, Jesus Christ.

You may be in a new season of life. Or there may be a place in your life that needs repair. You may be in the process of building or rebuilding, or it may feel like your life is in shambles. But, sister, God's plan isn't uncertain or incomplete just because your future or project is. Zerubbabel is on the scene. Not the Z of Haggai's day, but the ultimate Zerubbabel: Jesus, the Son, the Servant, God's Signet Ring. He has authority over your project in every season, so don't get discouraged by the process.

Take courage, my sister. Jesus is with you!

THE PROPHET, THE POLITICIAN, AND THE PRIEST

Joshua is in the house! So make room for him at your table or wherever you are studying today.

We're back in reoccupied Jerusalem again. We've got our prophet. We've got our governor. So who are we missing? The third character of the Book of Haggai. His name was Joshua. (Not the one who hung out with Moses and Caleb. Different guy.)

> Find Ezra 3:2 in your Bible and write down what this verse reveals about Joshua. (Remember, Jeshua is just a different spelling for Joshua in this verse.) Who was his dad and what did he and his brothers do?

The bottom line is Joshua was the high priest, and he was a descendant of Zadok (1 Chron. 6:1-15). He had been hauled away into captivity and now served as the religious leader of the community that returned to Jerusalem. Joshua reestablished the high priestly line of Aaron through Eleazar.

Now you've got a prophet, a priest, and a politician. And a complicated etymology and history lesson. Sorry. But think about it: a prophet, a priest, and a politician. Wow, what a combo! As you study Haggai, you'll notice that Haggai preached to the people. But he also directed his messages to the politician and the priest, the civil and the religious leaders of the people. It is as if Haggai recruited Joshua and Z to be his associates in pulling off God's plan. Priest, prophet, and ruler are all part of the way God spoke to and guided His people in Haggai. Is that still true today?

On the surface, it seems perfectly reasonable that God would guide and instruct His people through those who proclaim His Word, like the prophet and priest. But, usually, you don't throw a politician in that mix, right? Well, God used the political leader in Haggai's day, and He can use political leaders today, too.

Zerubbabel, the governor, was on board with God's plan. He was the signet ring after all. But not all political leaders are like Z. Can God use a political leader who doesn't seem to follow God's way?

Let's bring this home to our backyard. If you look back at America's history, you probably have opinions on who was a good president and who was not so good.

Can God use the not-so-good as part of His perfect plan? Read Daniel 4:17 and answer the following questions:

Who is sovereign over all kingdoms?

Who gives the kingdoms to anyone He wishes?

Who sets the "lowliest of people" in authority (CSB)?

No matter how high the office, no man is higher than the Most High. Think of it like this: America doesn't just elect a new commander-in-chief every four years to be president. God, the Commander of the universe, allows a person to be president. The Most High, our God, has got this! God is sovereign and in ultimate control, even over what seems totally crazy and out-of-control. God is ultimately in charge of those who are in charge—prophets, priests and, yes, even politicians (Rom. 13:1).

This is nothing new. It's been that way throughout history. Good kings, bad kings—all were under the rule of the King of kings.

One king who was part of Haggai's story proves this point: King Nebuchadnezzar. Everyone thought of King Nebuchadnezzar as the biggest, baddest king of his generation. And, in his mind, King Nebie thought of himself that way, too.

Read Jeremiah 27:1-6.

Describe what God called the vain king:

God called him "My servant." Sister, he sure wasn't God's servant in the way Jeremiah was, or in the way King David was, or in the way you and I want to be. He was pagan, pompous, and prideful.

So why do you think God called Nebuchadnezzar His servant?

The Hebrew term for *servant* that we see in Haggai 2:23 is common in the Old Testament. It's often used to describe people the Lord calls or uses for special service, whether they are followers of God or pagans.[13] It's a tough truth to swallow, but Nebie served as a tool of God's judgment of His people. In other words, God's perfect plan was pulled off by a bad king. Even a bad king was under the rule of the King of kings.

God has ultimate influence over the hearts of leaders who influence the future of nations.

When we realize that God has priests, prophets, and leaders—every one of them—in His hands, we can stop wringing our own. We don't have to be discouraged, no matter how bleak the national news gets or how dysfunctional the government is. Instead, we can take courage and march on "For the kingdom is the LORD's, and He rules over the nations" (Ps. 22:28).

There's a lot of wisdom in the way God instructed Haggai to address the people, isn't there? God wisely guides, corrects, instructs, and protects us today in the same ways. So trust His process.

Let's wind up this day of study with prayer.

Find in your Bible 1 Timothy 2:1-4 and use it to guide your prayer. In your prayer, include, as the verses instruct, petition, intercession, and thanksgiving for your leaders, both spiritual and political.

> Dear God,
>
>
>
> Amen.

Well, Session One is a wrap! Way to go, sister! You just won't believe how much we're about to learn together. Seriously, Haggai may be two little chapters, but it will be one big blessing in your life. Buckle up, sister, it's gonna get even better!

Love,

Jennifer

Notes

Group *session 2*

Welcome and Prayer

VIDEO NOTES

We have all had seasons of _____.

Our exile feels like we are _____ and not in the promised land we expected.

Ways we may experience exile:

- Sometimes our exile is _____.
- Sometimes the exile we feel is _____.
- Sometimes our exile shows up in our _____.
- There is purpose in _____.

Some of the purposes of exile:

- God may be allowing exile to _____ us.
- Another reason for our exile is that God could be _____ us.
- Sometimes God _____ us in exile.

Three Practices of a Woman in Exile:

1. _____ with your exile.
- Exile is about _____ not _____.
- _____ something.
- Increase in _____.
- Seek the _____ of our exile.

> Would you like to read my written summary of this video teaching? Just go to jenniferrothschild.com/takecourage

2. She pursues _____ in her exile.

- The only way you are protected from the lies in exile is to know the _____.

- If you do not know truth, you will not _____ a lie.

3. She is _____ with her exile.

- We need to be patient with _____.

- We need to show patience with the _____ of exile.

- We need to show patience with _____.

CONVERSATION GUIDE

Video 2

DAY 1: What stood out to you in your first read-through of Haggai? What did you find confusing? Encouraging?
When have you recently walked through a season of discouragement? What brought you low?

DAY 2: Do you ever feel like you are not useful in God's work? Why? How does Scripture combat those feelings?
What do you see as your current mission assignment?

DAY 3: How do you relate to the Jews' backstory of discouragement, despair, and fear?
We usually relate discouragement to a difficult season of life, but have you ever experienced discouragement during a time when things seemed good? If so, what does that tell you about discouragement?

DAY 4: When you see how God has woven the story of the Messiah through the Old Testament, what does that tell you about God?
How do you see God weaving you into His story?

DAY 5: How has God used different people to grow and shape your Christian life?
When you look back over your life, how do you see the sovereignty of God at work?

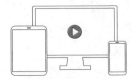

To access the video teaching sessions, use the instructions in the back of your Bible study book.

The Anatomy of Discouragement

MISPLACED PRIORITIES

Welcome to church, sister! It's sermon time! Haggai's book is made up of four sermons. Let's dive into his first one. I know you'll love it! Pour your coffee, and let's do this!

Turn to Haggai 1:1.

To whom was Haggai about to preach?

He's getting ready to influence the influencers—the priest and the politician. Remember them from last week? Z and Joshua were probably sweating in their sandals, wondering if they were being called on the carpet as Haggai began. The temple wasn't finished, and they were likely frustrated or discouraged. Haggai knew why.

Let's you and I skip down a few verses and start with the feelings before we tackle the facts. Read Haggai 1:6 and list the five reasons Haggai gave for their frustration.

1.

2.

3.

4.

5.

> Have you ever considered why we should separate our feelings from facts? Discover three ways I've learned to handle the hard facts of life on my podcast. Listen anytime at 413podcast.com/38.

What do those five reasons have in common?

It seems Haggai's people found themselves in the constant frustration of not enough. They found themselves in a state of perpetual disappointment. And discouragement. Nothing satisfied.

I'm sure we've all felt this way at some point.

Think of a time when you found yourself in a state of constant frustration or discontent. What were the circumstances?

What were the reasons?

Review Haggai 1:4.

Why did Haggai say the Jews were dissatisfied?

Paneled houses? Really?

Years ago, we had an old house with dried out, brown paneling. All I wanted to do was paint it or pull it off the walls! (This was BCJ—before Chip and Jo. They make things I would normally throw away look cool and attractive—and expensive). Our paneling was not very attractive or appealing. But "paneled house" doesn't mean to us what it would have meant to a newly-returned-from-exile Jew. To them, a paneled house was a sign of wealth. Walls and ceilings overlaid with cedar were common in wealthy residences back in the day. You can see this in 1 Kings 7:3,7 and Jeremiah 22:14.[1]

Understanding the meaning of "paneled house," what could Haggai have been saying was the true reason for their frustration? Circle which phrase best sums it up:

Unrestrained spending • Misplaced priorities • Bad taste in decorating

Let me give you a few questions to ponder as we think this through:

Is it wrong to live in a nice home?

Is it selfish to care about the appearance of your home?

Is it shallow to enjoy decorating your home?

Is it un-Christian to invest in a home?

Is it wrong to desire security and comfort in your home?

I ask you those questions because Haggai just got on to Z, Josh, and the people about their homes. Or did he? Hmmm . . .

Read Haggai 1:2-4 and tease out what the true issue was.

Timing seemed to be a big issue here. The word translated *time* in Haggai 1:2 means *a fit or proper time.* You may not see it in your translation, but the word *time* is used twice in verse 2. The repetition is used to show emphasis, and it also compares what the people say in verse 2 to what God says in verse 4 where *time* is found again. The people weren't saying that the temple didn't need to be rebuilt. They were just questioning if it was the proper time to do so.[2]

Dr. Stephen Miller states: "This pious sounding rhetoric was nothing more than an excuse not to follow the Lord. In reality many of the people had become so obsessed with their own lives that they had little time for the things of God. Moreover, in the following verses Haggai related that they selfishly would rather spend their money on lavish homes than the house of God."[3]

There's a time for everything. Investing in your home or in your needs or wants is not a bad thing in and of itself. But in Haggai, it seems that, as they say, timing is everything. Ponder that for a minute.

Which house was getting the people's time, priority, and attention?

Oh, girl, there's nothing wrong with living in a nice home, but there is something wrong with neglecting God's priorities while we pursue our own. The Jews' issue was misplaced priorities. And that's often my issue, too. We often can trace our discontent, discouragement, and dissatisfaction to a priority that is out of whack.

When self-promotion is above God-devotion, we end up dissatisfied.

In the case of the Jewish people, their self-focus involved neglecting to repair God's temple, therefore neglecting to worship in the temple. Girl, it wasn't about their houses; it was about their hearts. And, bam! Nothing has changed. It's the same with us, isn't it?

Let's think about a few things before we go on. Feel free to journal your thoughts under each question.

Am I generally satisfied and content? What do I do when I'm not?

Am I often seeking a greater thrill or different experience? If so, why?

What motivates how I spend most of my time?

Does my self-focus cause me to neglect what God has called me to do, or do I have a good balance?

Pause here and pray about your responses. When we study God's Word, we also need to study our hearts in the light the Word brings. So linger as long as you need to. Don't be in a hurry to just fill in some blanks, all the while leaving big gaps in your heart. Ask the Holy Spirit to reveal what you need to see about your priorities.

OK, good job. Your Father God doesn't want you to live dissatisfied, discouraged, or settling for misplaced priorities.

What does God tell you and the Jews to do about this in Haggai 1:5 and 1:7? What was the one command God shared in both verses?

The command is translated in different ways:

- "Consider your ways" (ESV).
- "Think carefully about your ways" (CSB).
- "Give careful thought to your ways" (NIV).

What do you think the command meant?

Go to your favorite Bible resource and try to find the original Hebrew meaning of the command. When you find it, jot down what it means.

The phrase "Consider your ways" is translated as *set your heart on your ways*. The word *consider* is a compound word composed of *set* or *consider,* and *inner man, mind,* or *heart*.[4]

The word translated "ways" is wait for it . . . wait for it . . . *ways!* Ha! Also, it can mean *journey* or *manner*.[5]

In the JRV (Jennifer Rothschild Version), it means, *In your deepest part, focus on what you do and why you do it."* Girl, we've got to consider our ways, set our hearts on our ways.

Have you ever "set your heart" on something? Suppose you and your BFF are meeting for dinner, and together you decided to eat at that new, Mexican place where they have the best *flautas*. Your mouth started watering that morning as soon as the two of you set the time and place. All day, you watched what you ate because you kept remembering the *flautas* for dinner. At 4 p.m. you were so hungry, but you decided to not snack at all because you were focused on those *flautas*. Now it's 5:55 p.m., just five minutes before she is supposed to swing by to pick you up, and she sends a text that says, "I had Taco Bell for lunch, let's get Italian instead."

You scroll through all the emojis that might communicate how that just can't happen. But, instead of a goofy image, you just text back with, "I had my heart set on Mexican. Suck it up, Buttercup!" OK, well, maybe not that last part. But you get the point. You had your heart set on Mexican. You focused on it. You were set like cement, determined and focused. Every choice you made leading up to dinner was made in light of what your heart was set on. That's what Haggai was saying: "Consider your ways." Set your heart on your ways, your priorities, your choices. Think about them. Pay attention. What is your heart set on? What is your priority?

Sometimes, we don't stop to consider our ways. We just do our thing and never stop to think about what we are doing and why we are doing it. We feel frustration or discontent and then amuse ourselves with something else and move on.

I want you to muse. Do you know what that means? If not, get a dictionary, find the word, and write the definition here.

Yep, it means *to think* or *ponder*. So what if you put that tiny letter *A* in front of it? If you do, you get *amuse*. Write the definition of *amuse*.

We all know what amusement is. If we get right down to the roots, *muse* equals *think*[6] and *a* equals *not* or *without*.[7] So to *amuse* means *to not think*. It means you don't consider your ways, you don't set your heart on your ways. You distract yourself instead.

So think about it today. Really consider your ways. Journal about what your priorities are. Consider where you spend your time, talent, and money—consider your priorities. Consider if and or where you feel frustration, discontent, or dissatisfaction in your life. Ask God to begin to refine your thoughts and give you clarity on how your priorities affect your satisfaction and contentment.

Lord, help us to consider our ways. Reveal truth to us. Amen.

Full day. Good stuff. See you tomorrow!

As you break down what causes discouragement over the next few days, listen to the Session Two songs of my *Haggai* playlist at **jenniferrothschild.com/takecourage**.

HALF-HEARTED DEVOTION

Yay! You're back! We are still in Haggai's first sermon today. I know I've skipped some verses here in chapter 1, and I'm about to do it again. Don't worry, we will cover them later.

For now, read Haggai 1:12-15.

What was happening in these verses?

Zerubbabel, Joshua, and the people obeyed and got busy working on the temple. Way to go, guys! They considered their ways and shifted their priorities. After eighteen years of neglect and frustration, the people aligned their priorities with God's.

How long did their shift in priorities last? Review Haggai 1:14-15. When did they start the work?

> ### MATTHEW 6:33 MOMENT
>
> The Jews had a Matthew 6:33 moment, and it made all the difference. Do you need a Matthew 6:33 moment? Read the verse and meditate on it. Ask God how that verse speaks to what you journaled yesterday about the ways your priorities impact your satisfaction and contentment.

Now, read Haggai 2:1.

What date was given?

This second date was the beginning of Haggai's second sermon, by the way. According to verse 1, it was the twenty-first day of the seventh month. If you do the math, it had been almost a month since the people began rebuilding the temple.

What did God, through Haggai, command in 2:4? What does this verse imply?

The wording seems to imply that the people were discouraged, and the work had slowed or come to a complete stop.

Haggai's message was that they take courage and get on with the work.

What was wrong with them? They couldn't even maintain for a month? I'd never do that! Ha! I wish. I am the queen of fresh starts and fizzling out. My Whole30® eating plan had to be renamed Whole13. And my New Year's resolutions barely last twelve minutes, much less twelve months!

Starting is often easier than finishing or maintaining, isn't it? (Unless you're a procrastinating perfectionist who can't ever start until you make sure you can do it perfectly.)

Why is it that starting is often easier than maintaining and finishing?

At the beginning, we are all in. Wholeheartedly committed and primed for the task. But then life happens, and we start to lose a little focus or get discouraged. Been there?

When was the last time this happened to you?

Let's "set our hearts on our ways" and see if we can figure this out. We will start with the heart.

Find Matthew 22:37 and list the three ways we are to love God:

1.

2.

3.

Jesus quoted from Deuteronomy 6:5 when He commanded us to love God with our hearts, souls, and minds.

Yet, look at your list. What is the one modifier that shows up in each of those?

Well, sister, it sure doesn't say we are to love God half-hearted or with some of our souls or with part of our minds, does it?

All.

When the people turned from the temple to their paneled houses, they were loving God with some of their heart, some of their soul, and some of their minds. But they weren't all in. They were distracted and divided. They weren't single-minded in their task because their whole hearts weren't in it.

Look at the list you made based on Matthew 22:37. Look at number one and number three. Number one comes before number three. Heart comes before mind.

I understand that most scholars state that the list *heart, soul, and mind* is not meant to be compartmentalized; rather it's to indicate our wholehearted devotion.[8]

However, I like to think God didn't drop a random list of words from heaven in no particular order. Seems to me there is good reason for the progression from heart to mind.

Why would it matter for heart to come first?

I contend that if your heart isn't fully devoted, you won't be single-minded. Your full attention will only be where your heart is fully devoted. That's why it's so easy to get distracted from our focus on God and His calling.

Single-minded living only comes from wholehearted devotion. If we are half-hearted, we will have divided loyalty and conflicted thinking.

What does James 1:8 say will be the result?

Sister, I need all the stability I can get, don't you? So how do we live wholehearted toward God so we will not be double-minded, distracted, and unstable?

Part of the answer is in Colossians 3:23. What word did Paul use to describe how we do our work?

What do you think "heartily" (or *from the heart* or *with all your heart*) means? (If you want to be ambitious, find the original Greek meaning in your favorite Bible resource.)

That word *heartily* means *with all sincerity*—in other words, with your whole self or from your soul.[9] It speaks of our motivation, our focus. We do our work heartily as unto the Lord. We do what we do with our whole selves, nothing held back, fully engaged, all-in, because we have considered our ways and lined up our priorities with God's.

Working hard and working heartily are not the same things though, sister. You can work yourself ragged with the wrong motives and come up short of the satisfaction you crave. You can be a half-hearted, unfocused woman who works hard but not heartily, and you'll still feel the constant ache of dissatisfaction and discouragement. God asks us to consider our ways and set our hearts on Him as priority. If your heart isn't all in, you are destined to burn out, wear out, or freak out when you face certain obstacles or opposition. You won't have the mental fortitude to keep on keeping on if your heart isn't fully devoted.

How would your life be different if you lived it heartily as unto the Lord?

What is one thing that needs to change for you to live with wholehearted devotion to God?

Now, turn what you wrote above into a prayer. We can have all sorts of great ideas and intentions, but without God's grace and power, we ain't got nothin'!

I'm praying for you and trusting that God is revealing your true heart and refining and encouraging you as you study. He's sure working on me!

See you tomorrow.

THE FRUSTRATION OF OPPOSITION

Well, hey there! Pull up a chair.

I'll open with a confession: I've got a pretty conflicted relationship with food. There, I said it. If you've known me or watched me from afar, you know this is because my size fluctuates. When I think about my haphazard history with weight loss and gain, I can easily connect the dots between when I am the least disciplined and the most discouraged. You know what I'm talking about if you have a similar struggle. When I am all in, wholehearted, setting my heart on my good-eating ways, I stay encouraged. When I am wholehearted, I am also single-minded. But, oh, sister, when I am double-minded and half-hearted, I end up frustrated and discouraged (and usually go up a size in my jeans)!

Sometimes, like me with my eating issues and the Jews with their paneled houses, we have misplaced priorities. The result is we lose heart, get distracted or discouraged, and sometimes even quit.

Yet sometimes we feel discouraged, and our priorities have nothing to do with it. Instead, our discouragement is because of other people's priorities. That's what we'll talk about today. We'll let Ezra the scribe guide our conversation.

Some parts of the Book of Ezra shed light on what happened before and during the time Haggai prophesied. We know that at some point between the time the exiles returned in 538 BC and when Haggai appeared on the scene in 520 BC, the work on the temple completely stopped.[10] (See the Haggai timeline on page 10.) The first few verses of Ezra 4 clue us in on what was perhaps the biggest factor on that first rebuilding effort being shut down.

> Read Ezra 4:1-5.

> Based on these verses, what factor contributed to the reason the Jews stopped working on the temple?

Here they were, working hard on God's house. Painting and plastering and doing their work heartily as unto the Lord. Giving it all they had. Then, their neighbors got ugly. The neighbors "set out to discourage" the Jews who were working on the temple (v. 4, NIV) Who were these people anyway?

What does Ezra 4:1-2 call them?

They were called *adversaries* (ESV) or *enemies* (NIV) of Judah. Those are some strong words.

But who were these people? Remember that the nation of Israel was divided into two kingdoms after Solomon's reign. The northern kingdom was made up of ten tribes, while the southern kingdom consisted of two tribes, Judah and Benjamin. Because of their continued disobedience, the northern kingdom fell to the Assyrians in 722 BC, and most of the population of Israel was exiled to Assyria.[11]

Find 2 Kings 17:24.

Describe what the king of Assyria did to repopulate the region:

The left-behind Jews ended up intermarrying with all the pagans who were settled in Samaria. The result? Samaritans. Yep, these enemies were the Samaritans. Even into Jesus' day, the Samaritans weren't popular with the Jews—to put it mildly.

Well, this was where it all started. The Jews didn't like the Samaritans because their faith was a combination of ritual from the Law of Moses and pagan superstitions. Their worship had a little bit of Yahweh and a little bit of anything and everything else. Most Jews in Jesus' time looked down on the Samaritans because they were religiously compromised. Theirs was a mishmash of Judaism and paganism. To supposedly worship Yahweh as one of many gods is not to worship Him as God at all.

And then, a couple of centuries later, these people were trying to discourage and put a stop to the Jews' rebuilding project.

Before the Samaritans "set out to discourage" the Jews in Ezra 4:4-5, they first tried a different tactic in Ezra 4:1-3. Circle which best describes it.

- They tried to hinder them.

- They relentlessly harassed them.

- They asked to help them.

- They tried to hurt them.

What did Z and Joshua say to their offer to help in Ezra 4:3?

Why do you think they refused the Samaritans' assistance?

The first time I read that the Jewish leaders said no to their offer, I thought, *Dudes, why don't you just use them to help? It will get the job done sooner!* But, for Z and Joshua, no was obedience. No was a reflection of being single-minded. They were wholeheartedly devoted to God and their calling. Saying yes to help from the Samaritans would have been a compromise. Oh, sister, may we never compromise what matters most for greater convenience to us.

Pause for a moment, put down your pen, and think and pray about that last statement. How does that truth impact or apply to you?

Z and J used wisdom in refusing what could have appeared as a sincere offer to help. After all, the Samaritans worshiped God . . . sorta. But to receive their help was to invite their influence. And to invite their influence was to endanger the purity and single-minded devotion of the Jews. After all, it was the Jews' idolatry that had gotten them into trouble in the first place.

We, too, must be wise in our relationships. You will encounter people who appear to be all in, but in reality, they are half-hearted. They may offer help just to eventually hurt. Some offer assistance so they can slowly influence you toward their way of thinking. A true adversary will be sneaky enough to show up as a friend.

In our relationships, we love all with the love of Christ, yet we also vet everybody through the wisdom of the Holy Spirit.

Sister, this is something we all need to really think and pray about. Sometimes no can be a response of single-minded obedience. We must pray continually for wisdom to see clearly and discern. If you're in a situation like this right now, keep 2 Corinthians 6:14-18 in mind as you consider how to move forward.

Obviously, Z and J made the right decision because the Samaritans' true motives surfaced in Ezra 4:4-5 after their help was refused.

Tomorrow, we'll look at more of Ezra 4 to see another tactic the enemy uses to discourage the people of God.

 Share your one sentence with your Bible study buddies and also with me on Instagram® or Twitter® @JennRothschild. Be sure to use the hashtag #TakeCourageStudy when you post!

> Until then, review and reflect on what you have learned today. Write one sentence to encapsulate what really spoke to you. Write it as if it were a Facebook® post. Include some hashtags to make it really clear.

#SeeYouTomorrow #You'reDoingGreat #WayToGoSister

THE STING OF ACCUSATION

Facing opposition seems to be a constant issue for the ancient Jewish people, doesn't it? Yesterday, we saw how the Jews were opposed by their enemies as they tried to rebuild the temple. This took place when Z, Joshua, and the other exiles first returned to Jerusalem, before the time of Haggai. Today, we're going to fast forward a few decades after Haggai, to the time when Ahasuerus (Xerxes), then Artaxerxes ruled the throne of Persia. We're about to see how opposition to the Jews reared its ugly head again as they worked to rebuild the city of Jerusalem. (See the sidebar on page 21.) I have a feeling you're going to relate to this situation. Maybe this should be a decaf day for you. I don't want you getting too fired up!

Pause to pour your coffee and ask God's Holy Spirit to guide you and be your Teacher as you read His Word.

> Let's start by reading Ezra 4:6.
>
> What did Judah's enemies do?

Accusation seems to be a favorite weapon for the enemies of God's people. In this situation, the enemy wrote a whole laundry list of complaints and accusations to the king against the Jews.

> Read Ezra 4:12-16 and see if you can pick out the crafty ways they accused the Jews.

Ezra 4:12	
Ezra 4:12	
Ezra 4:13	
Ezra 4:14	
Ezra 4:15	
Ezra 4:16	

When the opposition comes at you, trying to take you down and discourage you, the tactics are similar to what's found in Ezra 4. Falsely accusing and name-calling. Fearmongering and misrepresenting. Digging for dirt and dividing loyalties. Lies. Exaggeration. Attempts to isolate and diminish you.

Lies against you can cut to the core. It's hard to stand steady when your failures are exploited and your weaknesses exaggerated. When your character is attacked by slander and gossip, it's heartbreaking to watch influencers and teammates distance themselves from you. Accusation hurts.

> Has there been a time when you felt this sting? If so, briefly describe the situation and the hurt. If not, have you seen this happen to someone around you? Explain.

> Circle what was the most painful:

- **The lies**

- **The exaggerations**

- **The gossip**

- **The isolation**

My friend, if you or someone you love has experienced any of the attacks listed above, the pain from that situation is probably easy to recall. If that wound is still fresh or you still struggle with it at times, read Isaiah 53:2-11 and ask God to give you perspective and healing. Remember you have a Savior who understands that pain. He is "close to the brokenhearted and saves those who are crushed in spirit" (Ps. 34:18, NIV). Pause with the Scripture and ask the Spirit to comfort you and help you get some closure in this area. May you feel the honor of identity with Christ and rest in His strength and healing.

Accusation is a sharp arrow in the quiver of opposition. It hurts when it hits, and it causes all sorts of pain if it sticks. When we're unjustly accused and feel the press of opposition, we can get so discouraged, can't we? I sure can.

That discouragement isn't isolated to us or the ancient Jews. Check out these three Psalms and jot down phrases that describe the psalmist's despair.

Psalm 80:4-6

Psalm 88:1-9

Psalm 102:3-11

Those are quite the depressing lists, aren't they? The psalmist felt wasted, abandoned, and overwhelmed. He fought insomnia. His enemies reproached him. He felt isolated and alone. Ouch.

Oh, but that's not all! He said he had no strength, his heart was broken, and he felt forsaken even by God. Perhaps that was also how the Jews felt when their enemies set out to discourage them.

Accusation and opposition hurt. They *weaken our hands* as Ezra 4:4 reads in the King James Version. We feel like we can't hold on, that we're not strong enough for the task, and we want to just throw in the towel.

Oh, my friend, know this: when you get your priorities right and put your hands and heart to doing what God has called you to do, the voices of opposition will shout loud and long. You see, the enemy of your soul traffics in opposition. It may take the form of people who are jealous, unkind, threatened, or just plain mean. But make no mistake, it's of his doing. As Paul said in Ephesians 6:12—"Our struggle is not against flesh and blood" (NIV); Satan has a goal. And it is not to help you be who God calls you to be and do what God calls you to do.

His goal is plainly stated in John 10:10. Write it out here so you don't forget it! My enemy's goal is to:

How did Jesus describe Satan in John 8:44?

Satan is a liar and a joy-stealer. He seeks to destroy our work or reputation. He accuses and confuses.

So how do we handle accusation and opposition? Let's get really practical here. Usually the enemy uses words to hurt and oppose us. Sometimes the only thing that will give you the *umph* you need when the accusation is stiff, the opposition is rough, and the discouragement is deep, is God's Word.

I created my own "Scripture Pep Talk" to combat the enemy. You can do this, too! Honestly, when I am feeling beaten down, accused, and opposed, I sometimes can't even find the words to pray. So I give myself a truth talk. I personalize Scripture and put them together as a group to meditate on. An example is below. After you read through my list, write one for yourself.

The LORD is the one who will go before you. He will be with you; he
will not leave you or abandon you. Do not be afraid or discouraged.
DEUTERONOMY 31:8, CSB

Do not be afraid or discouraged, for the LORD
your God is with you wherever you go.
JOSHUA 1:9b, CSB

The LORD is with you mighty warrior. . . . Go in the strength
you have . . . Am I not sending you? . . . I will be with you.
JUDGES 6:12-16, NIV

Your strength will lie in quiet confidence.
ISAIAH 30:15b, CSB

No weapon formed against you shall prosper.
ISAIAH 54:17a

Therefore, there is now no condemnation
for those who are in Christ Jesus.
ROMANS 8:1, NIV

Finally, be strengthened by the Lord and by his vast strength. Put
on the full armor of God so that you can stand against the schemes
of the devil. For our struggle is not against flesh and blood, but
against the rulers, against the authorities, against the cosmic powers
of this darkness, against evil, spiritual forces in the heavens.
EPHESIANS 6:10-12, CSB

For it is God who works in you to will and to act
in order to fulfill his good purpose.
PHILIPPIANS 2:13, NIV

And the peace of God . . . will guard your hearts
and minds through Christ Jesus.
PHILIPPIANS 4:7

For God has not given us a spirit of fear, but one
of power, love, and sound judgment.
2 TIMOTHY 1:7, CSB

MY SCRIPTURE PEP TALK:

Well done! Take a picture of it and keep it on your phone so you can pull it up and say it out loud. And, girl, this is a dynamic document. Add to it as you face different situations.

If you're up for it, share your "Scripture Pep Talk" picture with me on Instagram® so I can cheer you on! Tag me @JennRothschild and use the #TakeCourageStudy hashtag.

Sister, God's Word is living and active. It is sharper than any weapon the enemy tries to wield. God's words are alive. But the enemy's and his minions' words are not alive; they are dead. They may hurt, but they are dead. Dead words can't destroy that which is alive in you.

When opposition starts to get loud, take courage and lean hard on God's Word and make His voice the loudest you hear.

> Finish up today by meditating on 2 Corinthians 4:16-18. Rephrase the passage into a prayer to God to help you be wholehearted in your faith and devotion so you can stand against discouragement. Ask Him to give you the right perspective on obstacles and opposition so that you do not lose heart.

Good job sister! God's got you, and I'm cheering you on!

SMALL THINGS SYNDROME

What a week we have had so far! We've considered our ways. We've chosen to be all in, wholehearted. We've walked in the Jews' shoes and felt the discouragement that comes from enemies who oppose and accuse.

It's hard to keep working heartily in the midst of opposition and accusations. But sometimes we're discouraged and lose heart, not because of outside voices but because of inside ones. Perhaps Haggai and his comrades also experienced this.

First, pause and pray: Lord, lead us into truth today. Be our Teacher and may we be doers of Your Word. Amen.

> Read Haggai 2:1-3.

> Based on these verses, what do you think the people were telling themselves about the temple?

Evidently, some of those who had seen the first temple reacted similarly when the foundation for the new temple was laid eighteen years earlier.

> Read Ezra 3:10-13.

> Describe the people's reactions:

While most of the people rejoiced, many of the older folks wept and were discouraged. For some reason, they felt the new temple was lacking in comparison to the old temple in all its splendor.

It's not enough. We're too small. Our stuff is too little. We're not as good. Ever felt those feelings? I call it "Small Things Syndrome" thanks to Zechariah. Let's welcome him into our Bible study.

Between Haggai's second and third sermon, Zechariah showed up with something to say.

Zechariah ministered at the same time as Haggai. He was a captive in Babylon, and returned to Judah when Cyrus released the exiles.

Read Zechariah 1:1-6.

What was His message to the people from the Lord?

Zechariah's message, similar to Haggai's, was to encourage the people to finish rebuilding the temple. He also saw that the people were distracted and disobedient. In this passage, he basically told them to "repent instead of repeat." In other words, don't repeat the sins of your fathers who disobeyed God. OK, you got a taste of Zechariah's message. Now, back to the people's perspective on the temple. Read Zechariah 4:10 below.

> Do not despise these small beginnings for the LORD rejoices to
> see the work begin
> **ZECHARIAH 4:10a, NLT**

What did God say about small things?

Judah's enemies looked down on the temple building as if it were Tinkertoys® in the hands of toddlers—as if it were no big deal. Even some of the Jews themselves thought little of the rebuilt temple because compared to the former temple, it was scrawny. But Zechariah, echoing Haggai (Hag. 2:3) reminded them it was no "small thing" in God's eyes.

Nothing is. No one is.

If you've ever felt small, like your mission, your age, or your work is just puny, let me tell you this—small things can have a big impact. Here's what I mean. Let's just take a small number and see if it can have a big impact . . .

Thirty-two isn't a big number, is it?

- Thirty-two little chocolate chips are only about seventy calories but will give you immense pleasure. (At least that's my personal testimony.)

- A thirty-two minute power nap may cost you about a half hour of productivity, but you will gain a new lease on your day.

- Thirty-two cents will hardly buy you anything. But if you save thirty-two cents every day for thirty-two years, you will have $3,737.60 in the bank!

- If you read thirty-two books over your lifetime, your brain will have processed more than one million words!

Thirty-two may be a small number, but it has big potential and big implications, doesn't it?

The Jews may have felt like they put in big work for little result. They may have felt small and insignificant because of all the opposition. They may even have felt that their best effort came to mediocre results.

Perhaps you identify with how they felt. You may feel small, insignificant, thinking who you are or where you are is unimportant compared to the seemingly big significance of others' lives and situations. But no one and nothing is really small and insignificant. The big impact of small things can be overlooked if we aren't careful. In a few weeks, you'll see exactly what this looks like in Haggai. You'll learn that you build more than you see.

Often, discouragement comes because we don't have a right-sized view of ourselves, our work, or our God. So let's check in with one last prophet, Isaiah, and see what he had to say about this.

Let's get the context. Turn to Isaiah 49:1. Who was Isaiah talking to?

Yeah, he was shouting at the distant islands and all the big people groups. And what was he saying? Warning: I'm going to ask you to do what Isaiah did in just a minute!

I shouted those words on a cruise ship balcony. I boarded the ship with far more than suitcases; I also brought some baggage of self-doubt and discouragement. I was in a season of feeling pretty beat up by life. So I stood on the balcony and pulled an Isaiah.

I stared straight into the boundless sea before me and said aloud, "Hey you, island! Before you became a clod of land out there, God knew me! He knew my name. Hey you, distant shore! I may feel awful small out here in this big boat on this big body of water, in the middle of these big problems I'm facing, but God knows my name. He knows me, not just about me. He knows where I am and how I feel."

OK, now it's your turn to pull an Isaiah! Lift your chin up, stand up straight, and quote Isaiah 49:1. Then paraphrase it to personalize it. It might sound something like this: "Listen to me, you islands; hear this, you distant nations: Before I was born the Lord called me; from my birth He has made mention of my name."

God does know your name. He doesn't overlook you just because somebody has a bigger problem, a bigger project, or a bigger personality. No matter how big the world is and no matter how small you may feel, God has called you to take courage and finish the work He has called you to.

That means, sister girl, that no matter where you are right now—whether you're in a transitional season full of uncertainty, feeling too small for your call, fighting opposition and feeling accused or discouraged, thinking you're too young or too old, or working heartily but wearing out—oh, girl, I have a word for you: take courage, dear heart.

God has called you to be the you He created. What you may see as a small thing in your mission or your work is really part of God's big plan. It was true for the Jews in Haggai's day, and it is true for you today.

Last thing, read Haggai 1:13.

What did God say to His people through Haggai?

God is with you in all situations and seasons just like He was with the discouraged Jews. God equips whom He calls. He lovingly corrects our "Small Things Syndrome" with His truthful words. He gives us the wisdom to consider our ways and prioritize our days. So, when you feel discouraged, don't give the enemy a chance to make it worse. Press into God's Word. Let His voice be louder than the outside voice of opposition and that nagging inner voice that tries to convince you that you are too small for your call.

OK? OK! Good job, you courageous woman! Two weeks down! Thanks for sticking with me. You're going to love what we learn next week.

Love,

Jennifer

Group *session 3*

Welcome and Prayer

VIDEO NOTES

The Samaritans were considered the _____ of Judah.

Samaritan Strategies

1. They seek to _____.

2. They seek to _____.

   • *To be discouraged* means that _____ has been removed from you.

   • The word *discouraged* is also translated as *weaken your* _____.

3. They _____.

4. They _____ your work.

Would you like to read my written summary of this video teaching? Just go to jenniferrothschild.com/takecourage

Video 3

DAY 1: When have you found yourself in a constant state of frustration and discontent? What caused it?

When have you seen your wrong priorities get in the way of God's purposes? What does it mean to *consider your ways*?

DAY 2: Are you quick to start something but struggle to keep working until the end? Explain.

What does it look like practically to love the Lord with "all your heart, soul, and mind" (Matt. 22:37)? Are you doing that? Explain.

DAY 3: How does our comfort and convenience tempt us to compromise what really matters?

When have you allowed a person or persons to influence you away from God or godly ways?

DAY 4: When was a time the enemy used accusation and lies to hurt you and hinder your spiritual growth? How did you deal with this attack?

How can the truth of Scripture help you keep moving forward, even in the midst of the slander?

DAY 5: Have you ever felt your work for the Lord is just a small thing of little importance? Why? And do you know now that it is not?

How can you encourage someone who feels the same way about what they are doing for God's kingdom?

To access the video teaching sessions, use the instructions in the back of your Bible study book.

The Antidotes for Discouragement

Day 1

DO THE NEXT RIGHT THING

Hey! You made it to Session Three. Way to go! Last week, we spent all five days dealing with the causes of discouragement. But this week, we look at the cure! Whew! I'm ready—how about you? We're moving forward, but we're staying in Haggai's first sermon.

> Turn to Haggai 1. Let's pause for a moment and ask the Holy Spirit to be our Teacher.

OK, I've poured the coffee, so pull up a chair, and let's chat. When my son, Connor, was just a little guy, probably about four years old, he had an independent streak. He always wanted to figure things out and do everything "by myself." So, when he encountered a problem, he would say with full toddler confidence, "I'm a solution-solver!"

God, through Haggai, was a Solution-Solver. In the part of chapter 1 that we'll look at today, He shared with His people what the problem was, and, more importantly, what the solution was.

> Last week, we discovered that paneled houses weren't the Jews' real problem, right? That was just a symptom. What was the real problem?

The issue wasn't their houses; it was their hearts. They had misplaced priorities. But God wasn't finished yet. He drilled down to the ultimate solution.

Read Haggai 1:7-9. Notice how Haggai pointed out the problem, the symptom of the problem (how the problem was hurting them), and the solution (how they could resolve the problem). Fill in the spaces below with phrases from the Scriptures that represent each element. Be aware, the answers don't appear in the order I listed. If you need a hint, the order they appear in is: solution, symptom, and then the problem.

Symptom of the problem	
The problem	
Solution for the problem	

The symptom of their problem was that they "expected much" and found little (v. 9, NIV). The people were disappointed in the return for their labor. They anticipated abundance, but instead the harvest was scarce, their incomes were low, and their standard of living was poor.[1]

What they brought home had slipped through their fingers. No matter what the people did, it wasn't enough. Their best efforts ended up as a worst-case scenario.

Often, we mistake the symptom for the problem. We think, *If I just had more, my problem would be solved.* Or *If I could just alleviate my frustration, my problem would be solved.* Nope. Your problem would be masked, not solved. "Not enough" was the Jews' symptom, the fruit, but it was not the problem. The root was the problem.

So what was the root? Any thoughts?

The Jews' problem was they were disobedient. They hadn't finished the Lord's house, yet they were busy building and finishing their own. Their disobedience led to dissatisfaction and discouragement.

The solution is found in Haggai 1:8.

What were the three things God told the people to do?

1.

2.

3.

The solution wasn't therapy with a plan to manage their symptoms; the solution was obedience. In summary, the three things represented doing the next right thing: "Go up to the hills and bring wood and build the house" (Hag. 1:8, ESV).

We need to understand that when the Jews first returned from exile, God had already supplied the wood—a special wood—the Jews needed to obey Him.

Let's find out more. Find Ezra 3:7 and answer the following from what you read:

Who was being paid to bring wood to reoccupied Jerusalem?

Where were the trees that supplied the wood coming from?

King Cyrus of Persia authorized the people from Sidon and Tyre to bring cedar wood from Lebanon to rebuild the temple.

Read the following passages and answer the questions to determine and describe why wood from Lebanon was important to the temple rebuild.

Read 2 Samuel 5:11; 1 Kings 5:6; 6:9-10,14-18.

How was cedar used?

Read 1 Kings 10:27 and Psalm 92:12.

What did cedar signify?

Cedar was used in the palaces of the kings and in the construction of the first temple. It was a symbol of wealth and luxury, but also of power and strength.[2] Yet cedar wood also signified something about God.

What does the reference to cedars in Psalm 104:10-16 suggest about God's character?

What does the reference to cedars in Psalm 29:1-5 suggest about God's character?

The fact that God planted cedars in Lebanon shows His provision, goodness, and beauty. The fact that He can break or burn them shows He is powerful and has authority to judge.

Cedar wood reflected God's character. He provided for the Jews what He expected from the Jews. He gave them what He desired from them. In other words, He supplied what they needed so they could obey Him.

OK, let me refill your coffee and tell you a story. When I was a little girl, my dad always gave my brothers and me money to buy Christmas presents for him and my mom. It was never much, just enough to find something we could wrap and put under the tree.

> As you discover the cure for discouragement over the coming days, listen to the Session Three songs of my *Haggai* playlist at **jenniferrothschild.com/ takecourage**.

When I was nine years old, I picked out two coffee mugs to give as presents to them. Seeing that it was 1972, my mom had a mug tree on our gold countertop near the avocado refrigerator in the kitchen with the orange beads hanging as curtains above the sink! The mugs weren't the height of mug fashion. But they weren't tacky either. Plus, they were purchased with thoughtfulness. I used everything my dad gave me to buy them for my mom and him.

Wouldn't it have been awful if on Christmas morning my dad opened my gift and exclaimed, "What is this? Cheap mugs?! Is that all you could get? At least you could have bought us nicer mugs to hang on the mug tree in our groovy kitchen!" I would have been crushed. Would that make any sense at all? How unreasonable and cruel it would be for a father to give only a certain amount of cash to purchase his gift and then scold the child for not having enough cash to purchase a gift that would please him.

My dad gave to me in proportion to what he expected to receive from me.

God gives to us what He expects to receive from us. Take a moment and personalize that thought.

Reflect for a moment. What has God given you?

Approximately fifteen years before Haggai came on the scene, God provided the cedar wood for the Jews to use to obey and honor Him (Ezra 3:7). But what happened to it? Perhaps that wood was used to panel their houses. If so, they took what God gave and used it for themselves.[3] Instead of doing the next right thing, they did the wrong thing with the right stuff!

> It would be like me spending the money my dad gave me on a new Barbie® doll. And Christmas morning, my father would have no gift. If that were the case, what would that say about me?

What would that communicate to my father?

When we take what God has given us and disregard it or misuse it, we are behaving like the Jews.

Consider what God has given you. Do you use it to serve you or to serve Him? Consider the following and journal your response or write a prayer to God in the space provided.

Your talent	
Your time	
Your health	
Your children	
Your home	
Your personality	
Your intellect	
Your relationships	
Your dreams	

Sister, do the next right thing with all God has given you—use the wood. Don't squander it. He gives you all you need to build His renown in this world.

Ponder today what symptoms you may be dealing with and ask God to reveal if "using the wood" is the solution you need. Sometimes discouragement and discontentment are the fruits of disobedience.

Remember, He gives you what you need to serve Him. So don't hoard or rebel or be afraid. Just take courage and do the next right thing!

Good job! I know this requires some heart probing, and I'm glad we're doing that together. See you tomorrow.

OBEY NO MATTER WHAT

Hey there! In yesterday's study, God, the Solution-Solver, showed the Jews their real problem by pointing out their symptoms. It sure made me think about the symptoms in my life that I need to consider. I hope you're doing the same.

Let's ask God to turn all those symptoms into mini-GPS units that lead us to the real problem. Rarely is the problem *out there*. Usually the problem is *in here*—in our hearts, in our choices, and in our priorities.

The people could have thought their real problem was that their houses needed paneling or that their crops needed fertilizer. They could have thought their real problem was that the new temple would be puny compared to the last one, so why bother?

But the real problem was disobedience. God's house still lay in ruins.

> Read Haggai 1:10-11.
>
> Describe the price of the people's disobedience:

> Now, contrast that disobedience with the blessings of obedience found in Deuteronomy 7:12-14.
>
> Describe what God promised:

This passage has a direct connection between obedience and blessing. Growth, prosperity, and fertility were all direct results of obedience. Death, poverty, and futility were results of disobedience. We may not see this in our gardens and barnyards like the Jews did, but we do experience it in our lives in different ways. When we're obedient, we experience spiritual growth and spiritual prosperity; we live in spiritual abundance. When we're disobedient, hope and peace die a slow death. We find ourselves in spiritual poverty, and our best efforts end in futility.

> According to Haggai 1:8, what is the purpose of obedience? Circle each answer that applies.
> - I obey to be blessed.
> - I obey to please God.
> - I obey to have a better life.
> - I obey to glorify God.

Ultimately, our obedience pleases God and is for His glory. Like John Piper says, "God is most glorified in us when we are most satisfied in Him."[4] That means that even if you don't see a direct link between your obedience and God's blessings, you are most blessed because your soul is most satisfied.

But can we be honest here? Sometimes in my most honest and flawed self, I hope, think, expect, and wish that my obedience will not only glorify God, but will also help me out a little! You know, like the Old Testament peeps, I will get the modern-day equivalent of better crops or fatter calves from my obedience.

> How about you? Do you sometimes obey God with selfish motivation, hoping for some physical rewards for your good behavior? Explain.

> Pause here and pray about this. Prayerfully journal the answers to the following questions:

> Does obedience guarantee blessing?

> Is blessing contingent on obedience?

Can it be true obedience if my motives are selfish or my heart isn't in it?

It's OK to want to be blessed or experience a better life. Often, God gives you all that in buckets! But here's the deal, sometimes obedience doesn't pay off—not in the way we expect. Hmmm . . .

OK, press pause. Time for a cup of coffee and some consideration. Put down your pen, lean back, and read this story.

In one of my favorite books, *These Strange Ashes* by Elisabeth Elliot, she recounts an African legend about Jesus. Let's be clear: this story is not in the Bible. It never happened. It's a made-up story. But the message sure does preach the truth. The legend hit me right in the heart and made me consider my ways—why do I obey the Lord?

Here's my version of the legend . . .

Jesus was walking along a rocky path with His disciples and asked each one to pick up a stone to carry for Him. They obeyed. Peter happened to pick up a small one, while John hefted a bigger one. Jesus then led them all up to the top of a mountain and, to the disciples' surprise, He turned the stones into bread. The disciples were hungry, so Jesus told them to eat the bread in their hands. Because Peter's stone was tiny, the bread in his hands was little—like a communion wafer. John's stone was big, so he had a giant loaf.

A few days later, Jesus and His disciples were walking another rocky path. Once again, He asked them to pick up a stone to carry for Him. This time, Peter picked up a larger stone— the biggest boulder he could carry. But Jesus didn't lead them up a mountain. He took them to the river instead. The disciples all stood on the bank wondering what in the world Jesus was doing. Jesus told them to throw their stones in the river. Each man obeyed. I can just imagine how Peter's eyes glanced between the water and Jesus, expectantly waiting for the miracle.

Nothing happened. They watched. They waited. Nothing happened except the stones sank to the bottom of the river.

No bread. No blessing.

Jesus, with great compassion, looked at His disciples and asked, "For whom did you carry the stone?"[5]

Wow, right?

Here's what I asked myself: for whom do I carry the stone? Do I obey Jesus for what I get out of it? Do I obey because I expect a blessing in return?

Have you ever asked yourself, "Can I really obey God no matter what?" That's exactly what we talked about on my *4:13 Podcast*! Listen in at 413podcast.com/86.

How about you? For whom do you carry the stone? Do you obey the Lord because it benefits you or because you just flat out love Him? Or is it a little bit of both?

Read Luke 6:46 and John 14:15.

What do these verses tell you about why you obey?

Sometimes we obey—carry the stone—because deep down, it serves us. But sometimes obeying God just isn't convenient—kind of like the Jews who preferred to finish their own paneled houses instead of God's house. Who wants to go up a mountain, gather wood, and build God's house when you've got your own fixer-upper that needs paneling?

Sometimes the weight of the stone doesn't serve our needs. We want the heavy tasks to become the bread that nourishes us. We expect the greater the obedience, the bigger the blessing. But, my friend, sometimes it just doesn't work out that way. Plus, that isn't the purpose of obedience.

For the Jews Haggai addressed, obedience was "go up into the hills, bring down lumber, and build the house." It wasn't for them. It was for God and His pleasure and glory.

We don't obey to get good stuff from God. We obey to give glory to God. We do it for Him, not for what we get from Him. We can find blessing in the process of obedience regardless of the outcome of obedience.

What blessings do you experience when you obey?

Does God sometimes bless obedience with tangible things? Sure. But most of the time the blessings are unseen—a closer relationship, a deeper trust, a growing love.

Is there an area in your life where you need to trust God and obey no matter the outcome? Explain.

Let's end today with prayer for grace to obey. I know I sure need it!

Dear God,

Amen.

Well, sister, you did some good stuff today. May we all be women who obey just because we love God and want Him to be honored and glorified. Yes!

TAP INTO OTHERS' STRENGTH

Coffee's hot, and so is our conversation today! So pull up a chair sister! We've talked about two remedies for discouragement so far. First, do the next right thing, or "use the wood." In other words, use what God has given you to serve Him. It will bring you encouragement.

Second, obey no matter what. Obedience will lift your spirit and bless you. But, girl, even if you're using the wood and obeying no matter what, you can still experience bouts of discouragement. Sometimes things just don't go well, or they're hard. Can I get a witness?

That's when you need a boost—a pat on the back, a card in the mail, a flower on your desk, a cheerleader to give you some good old-fashioned encouragement. One of the most obvious antidotes for discouragement is just that, encouragement. Yet, when we receive those words and actions meant to build us up, we need to recognize them and take courage from them.

The Jews in Haggai's day surely took courage from Haggai's and Zechariah's words and, of course, from God's presence (Hag. 1:13). Perhaps they were also able to recall the practical, tangible sources of encouragement that moved them forward when they first returned from Babylon years earlier.

That's what we'll talk about today (and tomorrow), and good old Ezra will help us. Turn to Ezra 1. Read through the chapter and put yourself in the Jews' shoes. Keep in mind they had been exiled in Babylon for decades. Their homeland and temple were in ruins. So while they surely were excited about returning home, the Jews must have also felt some anxiety about the destruction they would find and the rebuilding challenge they would face.

> Read Ezra 1 and pick out some things in the chapter that could have been sources of encouragement to these returning exiles (I found two).

1.

2.

Read Ezra 1:6 again.

What action is described in this verse?

The Jews' neighbors helped the returning exiles by supplying all sorts of stuff—silver, gold, livestock, and more—to the rebuilding project. "We're not sure whether their desire to help the Jews came from a desire to get in good with Cyrus or out of their own good will. Bottom line, they were generous."

When others offer their time, concern, help, money, thoughtfulness, or any other expression of generosity, it encourages us, right?

Go to your favorite Bible resource and read Ezra 1:6 in the King James Version. Jot down the result of the neighbors' willing gifts.

"And all they that were about them _____ _____

_____."

When you and I experience genuine encouragement, our hands are strengthened.

In Nehemiah 2:18 and Jeremiah 23:14, the phrase "strengthen their hands" implies invigorating or adding strength. But in Ezra 1:6 a teeny-weeny preposition is added in the Hebrew that slightly changes the shape of the metaphor. The image is that of grasping, laying firm hold on the hand with the view of strengthening or supporting.[6]

How does that refined image give a true picture of encouragement?

To me, that kind of encouragement is not just someone lending strength to you; it's someone becoming strength *for* you.

Can you think of a time or example when you've experienced that kind of encouragement? If so, describe how someone "strengthened your hands."

GO DEEPER

Who has been strength for you? Take a minute to send her a text, call, or even send a card letting her know how much she's encouraged you. Hearing from you just might be the encouragement she needs today!

Oh, girl, I sure can. On one of my lowest days, after dealing with a discouraging legal issue, my friends, Paula and Joan, marched through my front door and strengthened my hands. They washed my dishes. They turned up Michael W. Smith's "Surrounded," and we sang it at the top of our lungs! We sat in front of the fireplace and prayed together. By the time they left, my tears were dried, and I had a clean kitchen and a lighter heart! They became strength for me.

You may be in a hard season right now. Like the Jews, you may be facing rubble and ruin of what once was. You may be experiencing opposition, trying to do the next right thing but feeling helpless and hopeless. You may be in desperate need of encouragement. You just need somebody to strengthen your hands. Look around. You probably have people surrounding you who can become strength for you. But guess what? They can't be that if they don't know your need. So, right now, you are one of two people—either you are like the returning Jews and need strengthening encouragement, or you are like their nice neighbors, and you need to give strengthening encouragement.

Pause here and consider which one you are. (It's also possible you are both at the same time. That's been my experience before.)

Pray right now about your next step. Do you need to reach out for help? Sister, take courage. You have Bible study buddies who can strengthen your hands. Tell them. Ask them. Or do you need to reach out to help? Have open eyes and heart to see those who need you to be strength for them.

What actions will you take?

I will tell . . .

I will be honest with . . .

I will offer help to . . .

Sweet sister, God is the One who ultimately strengthens your hands. He is with you. He has a grasp on you and your situation. He has a firm hold on your life wherever you are and whatever you're doing. He won't let go of you. His grip will support you when you're weak. His presence is your strengthening encouragement. He won't just give you strength; He will be your strength.

Thank You, Lord, from the bottom of our grateful hearts!

PICK SOME MINI-CHEERLEADERS

I've got my mug of coffee, and I'm ready to jump into Bible study! How about you? Pour yourself a cup and pull up a chair.

Yesterday, we looked at the generosity of others as one source of encouragement. We affirmed how people's giving of time, talent, or help can strengthen our hands and encourage us.

Today we look at Ezra 1:7 to see the second source of encouragement.

Describe what was happening in Ezra 1:7-11:

Cyrus gave back the vessels from the old temple that King Neb had stolen. Why do you think getting back the articles from the temple would encourage the Jews?

Have you ever lost something precious to you and had it returned? If so, what was it and how did you feel when it was gone?

How did you feel when it was returned?

I know the feeling of losing something precious because my wedding rings were stolen. Ever since they were taken, I've wondered where they are, who took them, and if I will ever get them back. They were precious to me because they represented my most treasured relationship on earth. They also represented my identity and history. When they went missing, all the things they represented just felt off. It has now been a few years since they were taken, and I don't feel the depth of the emotion like I did at first. Actually, when I think about it now, my main emotion is pity and annoyance. Seriously, how could somebody do such a low thing? I now have a pretty but fake, inexpensive ring I wear instead. And I am totally fine with that.

But if my rings were returned to me? Oh my! I would be over the moon with joy and relief. I would feel like my history was slipped back on my finger where it belonged, my identity was back intact, and my gold and diamond were finally home.

Perhaps that's what it feels like to have precious things returned. It's more about what they represent than what they actually are. Perhaps the vessels that were returned were a big encouragement to the returning exiles and helped facilitate the rebuilding of the temple. They represented Judah's history and identity. They represented precious memories and reminded the people of God's presence and their sweet communion with Him.

Tokens from our past can serve as reminders of God's presence and faithfulness. Their encouragement in the present moves us toward the future.

> Take a moment to consider some of these kinds of precious things in your life. Maybe it's a photo, a book, an item, or a letter. What from your past reminds you of God's goodness and faithfulness and encourages you toward the future, and why?

THE POSSESSION	THE REASON

Perhaps the vessels of the temple had that encouraging effect on the Jews. The candle sticks, the basins, the bowls—these items all meant something to them. They may have been inanimate objects, but what they represented animated the Jews' hope and courage. The vessels from the temple became mini-cheerleaders that encouraged them to move forward.

Do you think it's OK for a material object to represent a spiritual lesson or provide spiritual encouragement? Explain.

Are material things necessary to have a spiritual experience? Why or why not?

Those precious items or objects from our past can be spiritual markers that cause us to ponder and praise the Precious One. We aren't dependent on these material things to have a spiritual experience, but they sure can serve as a reminder. This was the case for God's people even before Haggai's day, and it's still true for the church today.

Read the following passages and record how God used objects to remind, inspire, and encourage.

Joshua 4:1-7

1 Corinthians 11:23-26

Scripture also uses inanimate objects to represent the character of God.

In your concordance or online Bible resource, look up passages where God's character is represented by an inanimate object. Record the reference and the description. I've given you a few "Scripture Starters."

Scripture Starters
Psalm 28:7 • Psalm 62:1-2 • Psalm 91:2

God chooses relatable, material things to help us learn, understand, and remember who He is and what He's done in our lives. Material things shouldn't distract us from God; they can be used to attract us to Him. God is a Shield. A Rock. A Fortress. Bread and juice remind us of Jesus' sacrifice. You get the idea.

These things can become mini-cheerleaders that help us take courage.

A word of caution, though: remember that things are just things. They have no power. They don't provide us luck. They don't secure good fortune. They are reminders, pointing us to the One Who does have all power. If we attach too much meaning to an item, we create an idol. Yikes! No way! Don't let that happen, sister.

If you come to one of my "Fresh Grounded Faith" events, you'll see me holding my dad's preaching Bible on stage—I take it with me every time I teach. Post a picture of one of your mini cheerleaders and share why or how it reminds you of God and His character. I'm @JennRothschild on Twitter® and Instagram® so be sure to tag me and use the #TakeCourageStudy hashtag!

I gotta say, one of my most precious things is my dad's first preaching Bible. He left it to me when he left for heaven. It's precious to me because it reminds me of my father. I gain encouragement every time I hold it in my hands. Yet the most precious thing about that Bible is not who gave it to me, but who wrote it. God's Word gives me strong, unwavering encouragement and direction. It is a constant source of comfort and guidance.

That can be true for you, too, my friend. There is no greater encouragement than God's Word. When you take His Word seriously, you will take courage in this life no matter what you face.

On those days when you're weary in well doing or ready to throw in the towel, you can look on that precious thing and remember who God is and remind yourself of who you are—a woman who doesn't quit, always trusts, and walks with courage! Yes, that is you!

We're done for today! Good job, sister!

Day 5

LEAN INTO GOD'S PRESENCE

Wow! What a week!

So far this week we've examined a pretty sound to-do list to help us take courage when we're discouraged. (You know I can't help but review!)

1. **Do the next right thing.** Use what God has given you to accomplish what God has called you to do. If we spend all our talent, time, giftings, relationships, and dreams to serve ourselves, we'll end up in a paneled house dissatisfied and discouraged. That's why we need to line up our priorities with God's and do what He calls us to do when He calls us to do it.

2. **Obey no matter what.** Make your motive for obedience God's glory rather than your own blessing. We need to ask ourselves; *Will I still obey even if I don't get the blessings I hoped for?* When we obey no matter what, for the sheer love of God, we find courage and joy and fight discouragement.

3. **Tap into others' strength.** God puts people in our lives to bring us strength and encouragement through their generous giving of time, words, concern, or whatever.

4. **Pick some mini-cheerleaders.** Let precious things help you persevere. Ask yourself: *Are there objects in my life that represent God's faithfulness in the past and my identity in the present?* Allow precious things to be mini-cheerleaders that represent spiritual truths to encourage you when you are discouraged.

And, now number five …

5. **Lean into God's presence.**

Let's go back to the Book of Haggai. By now, you may have already spotted the two to three verses we will cover since we're talking about God's presence.

86   TAKE COURAGE: A STUDY OF HAGGAI

Skim the Book of Haggai and see if you can spot them, then write them out below.

Haggai 1:13 and 2:4-5 encouraged the Jews, reminding them God was with them. God's Spirit was abiding in their midst. Notice how courage and lack of fear were combined with God's presence in those verses. Why do you think that is?

"I am with you." This isn't just a statement of God's location; rather it shows His loyalty. God's presence is not about proximity. This phrase shows His commitment to us, His interest in us, and His investment in us. No wonder we can take courage.

Do a search in the Bible for the phrases "I am with you," "I will be with you," or similar statements. Jot down the references you find and what each verse suggests about the benefits of God's presence. (Or you can just use the "Scripture Starters" I found.)

Scripture Starters
Genesis 26:24 • Genesis 28:15 • Joshua 3:7 • Isaiah 41:10 • Jeremiah 1:8 • Jeremiah 1:19 • Matthew 28:20 • 2 Timothy 4:17

Based on the list above, write a note to yourself that you can read on your worst days to remind yourself that God is with you. Use the benefits of His presence that you listed as part of your encouragement to yourself.

> Dear Me,
>
> I know it's one of those days, but take courage, because God is with you.

Maybe you need to take a picture of that letter and keep it on your phone. It will help you remember that when you feel alone, the ultimate antidote to discouragement is the presence of God. The ultimate reason for courage is the presence of God.

God's presence means you will not be overtaken. It reassures you He is watching over you, and He is mighty to save. His presence calms your fears, strengthens you, upholds you, and helps you.

And, can we be honest here? If there were any group of people in history who could have just plain worn out God through their disobedience, faithlessness, and complaining, it was the Jews. (Well, OK, of course you and me, too.) But God did not abandon them. His covenant would not bend. His love would not walk away. His presence stayed with them.

His love will not walk away from you either. His loyalty will not bend. His presence is a constant for those who know Him.

If you're facing something bigger than yourself, if you are trying to pick up the pieces and rebuild, remember that He is with you. Those two words—*with you*—are two very powerful words that, when believed, can change how you face the day, the project, the problem, or the person.

As we wind up this week together, let's practice His presence intentionally. Perhaps you need to read your encouragement letter based on Scriptures about His presence that you wrote to yourself today. It could be you need to write the words *with me* on your hand or on sticky notes and post them everywhere. Maybe it's holding on to that precious thing you identified yesterday and letting it be a mini-cheerleader, reminding you of who God is and who you are and that you are never alone.

Or maybe you need to be part of God's strengthening encouragement for a Bible study buddy by sending her a text with the simple words, *God is with you.* Whatever it is, sister, do something today to practice His presence and feel the strength that comes from knowing He is with you.

I'll end the week with this verse I totally love and lean on. Paul told Timothy that at a time when Paul felt betrayed and alone that "the Lord stood with me and strengthened me" (2 Tim. 4:17a).

Sister, the Lord stands with you, too, and strengthens you.

All the way over here at my laptop, I'm standing with you and cheering you on, too! Way to finish Session Three! You're halfway there, so don't quit yet! Next session is full of even more good stuff!

Love you,

Jennifer

ENCOURAGING WORD

I hope you notice that one constant throughout this week of antidotes for discouragement is that everything we have discussed is found in, supported by, and built upon Scripture. God's Word is our consistent and life-changing antidote for discouragement. That's why we study it, meditate on it, memorize it, and live it. As Moses told the Israelites in Deuteronomy 32:47a, "For they are not meaningless words to you but they are your life" (CSB). Tweet me your favorite encouraging verse or life verse @JennRothschild. The Twitterverse needs your encouragement, and so do I!

Group Session 4

VIDEO NOTES

Sometimes _____ can lead to discouragement.

The prophet Jeremiah was called to what we might call a ministry of _____.

Jeremiah was proclaiming _____ that no one wanted to hear.

Jeremiah was _____ on God's Word.

Jeremiah was _____ to the ministry God called him to.

When we are discouraged, we can take courage because we were
_____, _____, and _____ by God.

Sometimes it takes courage to accept that we don't _____ His love;
we didn't _____ His love; we can't _____ His love.

The word *consecrated* means that you are _____ _____ for
something sacred.[1]

Your _____ is not dependent on you.

When you are given a calling, it means God has given you something that
is _____ _____ to do.

When you intersect your _____ with your _____, and you find
spiritual _____ there, chances are that's your calling.

> Would you like to read my written summary of this video
> teaching? Just go to jenniferrothschild.com/takecourage

DAY 1: In what ways do you struggle to be obedient to the Lord? Do you struggle more with the big things or the small things? Explain.

What are some resources God has blessed you with to serve Him?

How are you using all the resources God has given you to serve Him? Why is it so important to see yourself not as the owner but as the steward of those resources?

DAY 2: How have you experienced God disciplining you for your disobedience and blessing you for your obedience?

What is your motivation to obey the Lord? What should it be? If love is not your current motivation to obey, how can it be?

DAY 3: Why is encouragement so important in our spiritual lives? Share the most recent time someone encouraged you in the Lord.

When was the last time you were an encourager to someone? Why do we sometimes withhold our encouragement from others?

DAY 4: What's a token from your past that reminds you of God's goodness and faithfulness? Why is it important to have those things? Why is it important that we keep those things in the right perspective?

DAY 5: What are the many benefits and blessings of God's promise to always be with us? Do you really believe that God is present with you? If not, what's causing this doubt?

To access the video teaching sessions, use the instructions in the back of your Bible study book.

The Actions of Courage

Day 1

AVOID THE COMPARISON TRAP

Welcome to Session Four, you amazing, courageous woman! Except for some quick dips into Haggai's second sermon on Day One of Session Two and Day Five of Session Three, most of our focus has been on Haggai's first sermon. Now we say, "Amen" to it and move on.

Let's jump into the second sermon with both feet.

Turn to Haggai 2:1-9. Before you read the passage, pour some coffee or tea and ask God's Holy Spirit to be your Teacher. Amen.

> Now, read the entire passage but hone in on Haggai 2:1-3. That's where we will hang out today.

> Jot down when this sermon was preached according to Haggai 2:1:

Haggai preached this sermon "In the seventh month, in the one and twentieth day of the month" (KJV). Oh, sister, I am no math girl, so when numbers start flying, I duck and run for a book cover!

> But if you like all things digit, look back to Haggai 1:1 and determine how much time has passed since Haggai's first sermon:

By our modern calendar calculations, Haggai's first sermon was preached on August 29, 520 BC, and the second sermon followed on October 17 of the same year.[2] So there were around seven weeks in between the messages. For a moment, think about what you have been doing over the past seven weeks. You've been busy, right?

> Go back to Haggai 1:14-15 and determine what the Jews were doing and for how long:

Haggai preached his second sermon almost a month after the people started their work on the temple. So, at that point, they had considered their ways and prioritized their days. They had done the next right thing and obeyed no matter what. Despite the demands, desires, and distractions of their daily lives, they had followed their calling and begun rebuilding the temple. When we're living like that, it's all good, right?

Hmmm . . .

Evidently not. Something's going on in Haggai 2:3. What seems to be the problem Haggai referred to?

As the second temple was beginning to take shape, a group of the older Jews became discouraged. These senior citizen Jews had seen the size and grandeur of the first temple before they were dragged off into exile. They were now comparing the new temple, Zerubbabel's temple, to Solomon's temple. Zerubbabel's temple was built on a smaller scale with a smaller budget. There was just no comparison!

Comparison is a trap, and it takes courage to avoid it. But it also takes wisdom.

Pause and ask God to give you wisdom as we deal with this issue.

Unfortunately, we sometimes have the same tendency to compare like those older Jews. Smack dab in the middle of the demands and distractions of our daily lives, we still are able to fulfill our callings and then . . . bam! We look back and compare today to yesterday. We compare how we think things should be to how they actually are. We compare our gifts to her gifts, our calling to her calling, our church to their church. And we can end up feeling like a nobody with nothing!

How did the Jews view Zerubbabel's temple in light of Solomon's (v.3)?

Kind of Small • Somewhat Adequate • Like Nothing • Good Enough

Nothing. Nada. Zippo. They said it was "like nothing." Ouch.

Have you ever visited someone's grand and beautiful home and then walked back through your own front door and fallen straight into the comparison trap? Compared to that HGTV® model home, your house seems "like nothing" to you. But is your house really like nothing?

You get the idea.

Was the temple really nothing? No. It already had an altar and a foundation (Ezra 3). And the people of Haggai's day had begun to rebuild on that. It was something, right? Think about that as I tell you what happened while I was writing this week of study. I couldn't believe the timing.

When I was working on this study at the writers conference at Lifeway (the publisher) with a great team of partners in ministry, I learned that a million—literally, not just using hyperbole—of my Bible studies had been sold over the past ten years. Because I am so number challenged, I had no idea. We all celebrated with chocolate chip cookies and joined in prayer to thank God. (If I had known you get chocolate chip cookies, I would have paid more attention!) Anyway, on the drive home, I called my girlfriend to tell her. She whooped and hollered in celebration. But when she calmed down, she said, "Compared to some other Lifeway authors' sales in one year though, it's like nothing."

Now, sister, don't get upset with her. Her comment wasn't meant to be discouraging, and to me it wasn't. I love this woman and know she's got my back. She just doesn't have a filter! I never have to wonder what she's thinking because she says it out loud! But can that kind of comparison leave an author discouraged? Of course, it can!

But here's the deal. That million sold—it is something. It represents the goodness, grace, and faithfulness of God. And it represents a million women who I've been able to study God's Word with! It may be different than the something God gave another author, but it is not nothing. However, it can feel like nothing if I choose to compare. That is the point. Using someone else's gifts or calling is a crooked measuring stick. If I use those things to compare, then my flesh wants to rise up and compete. My motives get all messed up. And *that's* why comparison is a trap.

So what comparison bait pulls you into the trap? It could be your gift, job, or calling. It could be your success or appearance. It could be comparing your performance today versus when you were younger. Or maybe it's your accomplishments versus your way-too-high expectations.

 As you learn how to act with courage this week, listen to the Session Four songs of my *Haggai* playlist at **jenniferrothschild.com/ takecourage.**

Be honest here. What is your "something" that feels like "nothing" when you compare it?

I mentioned that one of my responses to comparison is competing.

Take a moment and consider how you respond when you're in the comparison trap. You may become very critical. Or perhaps you push yourself to work harder and harder. Or maybe you fall into discouragement, even despair. What is your typical reaction when you start to compare and come up short?

We girls need to be honest with ourselves and God. What we aren't honest about, we will never be free from. And what we don't admit, we permit the enemy to use against us.

Pause here and pray. Write out your prayer admitting where you are vulnerable when it comes to comparison. Confess how you typically respond when you fall in the comparison trap. Then ask God to help you see things from His perspective and give you courage to walk in this truth.

Dear God,

Amen.

The people were discouraged and weepy because they were comparing the new temple to the old one. They compared the past to the present. They looked at what God did then and compared it to what He was doing now. They used the wrong measuring stick and came up short.

What blessings could you miss if you use the wrong measuring stick?

What do you think a right measuring stick would be?

Consider this: what if you compare who you are and what you do to who God called you to be and your obedient response to that calling? What if, when you feel yourself slipping into that comparison trap, you measure your behavior, motivation, or activity against the standard of wholehearted obedience?

Look back at your "like nothing" areas of life and ask yourself:

Have I obeyed the Lord?

Am I following His call in my life?

Am I being the "me" God created and called me to be?

Is my heart wholly devoted to Him?

If you answer yes to those questions, then, sister, turn those tears of discouragement into tears of joy. Remember, it's not the outcome that determines our satisfaction—it's our obedience.

The real danger of comparing is possibly missing the real glory. Looking at our lives, callings, and work with eyes of comparison means we can't see with eyes of faith. It was true that Zerubbabel's temple was not as outwardly impressive as Solomon's. However, in a few verses (and weeks), we'll see that Zerubbabel's temple was to have a greater glory that the people couldn't see at the time. The temple that brought out their disappointment was the temple of Jesus' day. We'll dive deeper into this in the last week of our study. Just wanted to whet your appetite.

Look at Haggai 2:9 again.

What was God's response to the people's comparison?

God declared that this temple would end up being greater than the greatest one the weeping Jews could remember. God was doing His own comparison, but His perspective was totally different.

What does that say about your ability to do accurate comparisons?

We can't always see the full potential of something while we're in the middle of it. We can't see how the seeds planted by one small act may grow. We fall into the comparison trap and end up stuck in discouragement because we compare what we see to the wrong things.

What if, instead of comparing, we look at our simple act of today's obedience in light of what God can do? What if we look at our wholehearted devotion in the light of the promises of God? The result will be courage instead of comparison.

So, sister, choose the right perspective. See things clearly through God's eyes rather than the foggy lens of comparison.

OK, enough said! I don't know about you, but the Holy Spirit did a work on my heart today! I need more coffee . . . or a nap! Thank You, Lord, for being our Teacher. Amen.

See you tomorrow!

FIND YOUR ONE THING

Hey there! Yesterday's study was so convicting to me. How about you? I can relate to those older Jews who wept—not because I'm old or anything (wink)—but because I overlook true blessings of obedience when my eyes are on the wrong things. Today, we'll move to the next verses in Haggai 2 and see how God handled the weepy elders who were disappointed and discouraged.

Review Haggai 2:1-3. Then, read verse 4.

What was the one little four-letter verb or action word in Haggai 2:4 that God used to tell the Jews what to do next?

Grab your dictionary and write the definition of *work.*

Do you work outside the home? If so, what is your job?

If your work is not outside the home or if you don't work in a professional capacity, what do you do with your time? (Because I know you work, sister!)

What do you like best about the work you do?

Is your work identical to your BFF's, spouse's, or neighbor's work?

Of course not! Sorry for the dumb question. But I am going somewhere with this. *Work* is defined as our *exertion or effort to accomplish something.*[3] There are a million ways to do work and a million different jobs, talents, skill sets—everybody has different things they do well. Your BFF may work in accounting. If you're married, your spouse may be a truck driver. Your neighbor may be a nurse, a gardener, a teacher, a cook, or a cashier. You may be a CPA, LPN, PhD, or MD. Or you may be a homemaker and a homeschool mom. Everybody has a different job. Usually, we gravitate toward particular work based on our particular skills, talents, or interests.

What is the main reason people work?

Besides providing income, I think the main reason people work is that it gives them a place to do their thing—to do what they're passionate about, called to, enjoy, or skilled at. Sure, there are times we don't love our jobs, but we're grateful for the opportunity to contribute to supporting our families and serving others.

Now, here's my question: If you could wave a magic wand and be able to work in whatever field you wanted, what would you do and why? (Of course, it may be what you are already doing.)

Chances are what you wrote down reflects something about you. It likely reveals your one thing. You know, that thing you care about the most, what you're the best at, and most passionate about.

Well, in Haggai 2:4, the Jews had a chance to do their one thing. But their one thing finds its context and purpose in the main thing. Based on what you have already learned about Haggai's prophecy, what was the main thing God was calling the Jews to do?

Yep, the main thing was building God's house so that He would be glorified. Get practical in your thinking here. In order for the main thing to happen, the people had to apply each of their "one things" to the job. Somebody hammered. Somebody did the drywall. Somebody swept up sawdust. Somebody made PB&J and lemonade. You get the idea. Many parts but one purpose.

Does that remind you of anything you've read in the New Testament? Hmmm . . .

> If you're not sure, here's a hint. Go to your favorite Bible app or Google® and type in "one body verses" and list some Scripture references that pop up.

I found a few. First, Romans 12:4-5 declares two distinct truths that inform our one things.

> Circle the statement not found in those verses:
>
> • We all have different functions.
>
> • Some of us have more important positions and functions in the body than others.
>
> • We all function in conjunction with each other.
>
> Do you believe that some of us have more valuable positions or functions than others in the body of Christ? Don't give me a head answer, give me a heart answer.

> Let me ask it this way, do you believe that my one thing may be more valuable or necessary than your one thing? Explain.

Oh, my sister, I sure hope you wrote a big NO WAY in all caps! My one thing is not more important or more valuable than your one thing. God gives us all different giftings, and each gifting matters and is necessary to accomplish the main thing. In fact, my one thing couldn't occur without Paula, Marta, Denise, Val, and Mike doing their one things. (I would run out of space if I listed everybody.) All of our one things matter. The ground at the foot of the cross is perfectly level. No one has a higher status than anyone else. Nobody's one thing is a bigger or better thing.

ENCOURAGER SHOUT OUT

Who are the people in your life who help you do your thing because they do their thing so well? Pause and give them a shout out on social media using the #TakeCourageStudy hashtag. (And tag me, please, so I can like it!) Or text, call, email, or write a note to say thanks and encourage them today. "Encourage each other daily, while it is still called today" (Heb. 3:13, CSB).

Let's go to another Scripture. Read 1 Corinthians 12:12-20.

What was Paul's point in differentiating the unique body parts, like eyes and feet and ears?

How does 1 Corinthians 12:20 apply to this idea of each of us having a one thing that leads to accomplishing the main thing?

Girl, the point of your one thing is to contribute to the main thing. You may think that what you do in the body of Christ is of little value. It may be behind the scenes where no one notices. But I promise, what you see as little—what the world may see as little—God sees as mighty. The church needs all of us doing what we're called to do to accomplish God's purpose. You may think it's no big deal, but to God and His church, it's a big deal!

You may need to hear with your heart what God said through Haggai: "Take courage and work; for I am with you" (2:4, NASB). Take courage. Be brave and do what God has called you to do. You may have to persevere through your doubts and shaky confidence to do that thing. The enemy may try to devalue you, distract you, and discourage you, but don't take that nonsense from him! Instead, take courage and do what God has designed you to do.

Remember, no "Small Things Syndrome" for you and no crooked measuring sticks!

What is your one thing? Do you know? What is your spiritual gifting? What are your talents? What are you passionate about? Those things will help you know how God wired you to serve Him. Look back at that personal mission statement you wrote on page 16. It might help narrow your focus.

But keep this in mind—your one thing may look different at different seasons of your life. For example, you may be gifted to teach. But how, where, and to whom could change through the years. Or, your one thing may be hospitality. Yet, in your twenties that could look like inviting neighborhood moms over to your messy house for a play date. In your forties, it might look like a catering business that helps you financially but is also used to minister to people in crisis. No matter what season of life, if hospitality is your one thing, you're probably quick to organize the meal train for the family who has a newborn, and you're the first to jump over a pew to welcome the first-timers who visit your church. You get the idea. Maybe it's not just one task, but one theme you need to pay attention to. Whatever it is, be faithful to what God has called you to and gifted you for.

Take a moment to journal your thoughts or write out a prayer asking God to clarify this for you.

Sister, if you aren't sure what your one thing is, don't let that overwhelm you. It may not be just one thing, but your giftings and passions may all fall into one theme. It may take some time to discover it. But all the while, do the most important one thing. John Stoughton put it best when he wrote: ". . . a communion and fellowship with God, which is that *one thing*, which if a Christian had, he needs desire no more."[4]

Walking with God on the path He leads you on is your most important one thing. So take courage, my friend, and take a step! Do your one thing in the big scheme of all things God is doing to accomplish His main thing in this world.

Be brave enough to be you and do what God is calling you to do! I'm cheering you on!

Day 3

LIVE STIRRED UP

I've poured my coffee and pondered Haggai and all we're learning. I couldn't keep plowing through Haggai's second sermon without pausing for some clarification. So pour your coffee or tea and read Haggai 2:4 again.

You know that four-letter word we talked about yesterday? Well, I'm afraid I'm setting you up for failure without a little context. You could read Haggai 2:4 as an isolated imperative—work, work, work—or a pull-yourself-up-by-your-boot-straps-and-get-with-it kind of command. Then, twenty minutes later, you will be taking Tylenol® instead of taking courage because you'll be worn out with fatigue, frustration, or failure.

Imperatives without empowerment are impossible.

I want us to see what God did for the Jews in Haggai 1, which empowered them to do the work of rebuilding the temple. We need this help from God, too, if we are to follow Him and fulfill His purpose for us.

Read Haggai 1:14.

What did God do for Zerubbabel, Joshua, and the people?

Look in your favorite Bible resource for the original Hebrew for "stirred up" or "roused." Jot down some of the other meanings you find.

Now, use each word or phrase you found to complete the following sentences.

God _____ so I can do His will.

God _____ so I can follow His calling.

God _____ so I have the power to do what He asks.

God _____ so I will keep doing my one thing and not quit.

In case you didn't or couldn't look up the Hebrew, here are some original meanings: *arouses, awakens, lifts up, opens eyes,* or *stirs up.*[5]

Did you get the big idea here? Once God stirred up the people, they started the work. It is the same with us. We need God to stir us, rouse us, and awaken us. Let me show you what I mean.

Find the following Scripture passages and describe God's role in each:

Philippians 1:6

Philippians 2:12-13

In each of those verses, the word translated *work* is derived from the Greek word *ergon* which means *to work or accomplish.*[6]

Forms of that Greek word also show up in Philippians 2:30 and Philippians 4:3. Read those verses also. I'll wait.

What did you notice about God's work and your work?

Paul used several forms of that Greek word *ergo* to describe both God's work of salvation in us and our work of obedience that flows from His empowerment in our lives.

When speaking about both the work of God and the work of the individual, one of my former (I won't call him old) college professors, Dr. Richard Melick, says: "Paul recognized the place of each. Divine initiative called for a human response. While he believed that, ultimately, all of salvation, considered in its broadest scope, depended on God's initiative and power, he never tolerated passive Christianity. Human energy could never accomplish the work of God, yet God did not accomplish his purposes without it. The two functioned in perfect harmony, and people cooperated with and contributed to what God did in them and in the world."[7]

Sister, God begins the work in you. God works in you to will and work for His pleasure. You work out your salvation and do the work of Christ because God is at work in you. Got it?! Whew! God stirs us by His Spirit, and we respond with obedience.

> Find the following verses and describe how each verse expresses this concept. Be prayerful and patient with this because on the surface, the passages may seem to have nothing in common. But, sister, they all express the connection of God's stirring and our starting.

Psalm 51:15

Psalm 127:1

Romans 15:13

David knew he couldn't worship unless God opened his mouth and gave him a voice. Solomon knew he could hammer all day, but it would come to nothing unless God built the house. And Paul knew the Christians in Rome couldn't overflow with hope unless God filled them with it in the first place.

Sometimes we live in defeat and discouragement, because we try to pull off the work in our own strength and on our own terms. We try to do our one thing in our own power. We try to start up without being stirred up, and we stall out. Then, we end up sitting out on what God has given us to do.

Is there something you've been trying to do for God in your strength alone? If so, what is it? How's that working out for you?

Read Zechariah 4:6.

Now, personalize it to apply to what you just wrote. Rephrase it into a declaration that you will do what you do in God's strength with His stirring.

Girl, it is not by your power or might; it is by God's Spirit that you will accomplish the work He has for you. You give Him your grit; He gives you His grace! So, how do we live stirred up by God's Spirit every day—even on Mondays?

God's Word. You can't live stirred without His Word!

I know that sounds like a simple little rhyme but, sister, it is the profound big truth. So, maybe if you say that statement to yourself, you'll remember how to live stirred up. Go ahead, no one's listening but me.

You know why that statement is true? Because God's Word is "alive" (Heb. 4:12), and it gives you life. And, it's "active" so it can activate God's plan and purpose in you. (By the way, the Greek word for *active* is also derived from *ergo*.)[8]

When you feel stagnant or stuck, let this jingle sound in your heart: I can't live stirred without His Word. Then, take your Bible and open it. Read it. Meditate on it. Memorize it. Pray it. Trust it. Live it.

OK, last thing. Read 2 Timothy 1:6.

Describe what Timothy was supposed to do when it came to his calling, his one thing:

Paul wasn't saying Timothy's spiritual fire was petering out, just that Timothy was to fan the flame—keep on keeping on—and use his gift for ministry. If you know Christ, God has gifted you for ministry, too. That giftedness isn't to lay dormant in your life, but to be used in the stirring and power of the Spirit.

Do you want to live stirred up? I sure do. I don't just want it; I need it. Write out a prayer of confession and commitment to God about this.

Dear God,

Amen.

Girl, God's got a purpose and plan for you that He designed for you to walk in, so stay in His Word and stir up that gift in you by doing your thing!

Amen and amen. Well done. See you tomorrow.

RESPONDING TO GRACE

My friend, if you want to live stirred up, you need to be raised up! Without Jesus bringing you to life—saving you—you are still dead in your sin. Is that you? Dead in sin with no power to accomplish His purpose? If so, now is the time to change that by responding in repentance and faith to God's offer of salvation. Read Ephesians 2:1-10. Talk to a Bible study buddy right now. Tell her your need so she can help you respond to God's grace. Then, filled with God's presence and power you can live a life of peace and purpose in Christ. If you do this, please let me celebrate with you. Tweet me @JennRothschild. I can't wait to give you an emoji hug!

Day 4

REBRAND EGYPT

Hey there, sister! Are you all stirred up? I am praying for you. I'm asking God to keep you encouraged to be who He created you to be and do what He calls you to do. Live stirred up while you stir up that gift of God that He placed in you.

We're moving to Haggai 2:5. So settle in, take a deep breath, and ask God to be your teacher today. Amen.

Now, review Haggai 2:1-4 and then camp out on verse 5.

Here's a glimpse into how I do Bible study. Feel free to follow my lead. First, I pray and read the verse several times. So go ahead and focus on Haggai 2:5.

Then, I start with what lies between the punctuation. In other words, I go phrase by phrase.

Break this verse into three parts—the three phrases that fall between the commas and semicolons and periods. This will make understanding the verse less intimidating.

Let's start with the first phrase. Here it is in some different translations:

- "This is the promise I made to you when you came out of Egypt" (CSB).
- "According to the covenant that I made with you when you came out of Egypt" (ESV).
- "This is what I covenanted with you when you came out of Egypt" (NIV).

Now, what questions come to mind when you read that first phrase? Jot them all down!

Here are mine.

- Who was in Egypt?
- Why were they in Egypt?

- What was Egypt like?

- When did they come out of Egypt?

- What did God covenant to do, or promise the people when they came out of Egypt?

Did you notice we can't move forward without going through Egypt first? (We'll get to the covenant part in a bit.)

Words are powerful. Certain words probably cause you to recall a memory, elicit a reaction, or experience a strong emotion. Sometimes our strongest associations are negative ones.

GO DEEPER

If you've ever wished you could study the Bible on your own, you can! Stopping to ask questions as you read Scripture is a great way to go a little deeper in your understanding of the verses you're reading. The Bible study resource list in the back of this book is a great starting place to help you find the answers to your questions.

For example, I haven't eaten a Three Musketeers® candy bar since I was in the fourth grade. There was one in my Christmas stocking that year, and I swallowed it in one big gulp. Within minutes, I, uh, well, I unswallowed it! You get the gross idea. To this day, I associate that candy bar with . . . well, you know!

As I am writing this, I realize I have an issue with another word that represents a lot of fear and stress. This fall, I have a speaking opportunity in a city (which shall remain unnamed) where I've spoken before. The last time I went to that city was a travel nightmare. I got stuck in the Dallas airport overnight alone, both going and coming. I had to get to hotels in Dallas by myself, blind! I got some help from the airport personnel and hotel employees, but, girl, getting that help took hours. Enduring that stressful process twice still leaves me shuttering with fear. Now, whenever I hear the name of that city, my body reacts with stress! See what I mean?

What are some words that produce a negative association for you?

WORD	WHY

For the Jews, the word easily could have been *Egypt*. Why do you think that might be?

If you recall, the Jews' ancestors were slaves there. Skim through Exodus 1 and list some of the words that describe the Jews' time in Egypt.

Slave labor was their daily life. The Jews were treated ruthlessly and were constantly oppressed. Their lives were bitter. Even their baby sons were threatened, and probably some were killed. (And I thought my traveling alone story was a nightmare. Ha!)

These Jews had every reason to feel dark emotions and remember negative stories when it came to the word *Egypt*.

Egypt was slavery. Egypt was pain. Egypt was sorrow and loss and hardship. If Egypt was a brand, the Jews would avoid it! That's why God, Who redeems everything, rebranded Egypt for the Jews in Haggai 2:5.

How was God framing Egypt based on Haggai 2:5? What association was He prompting the Jews to make when it came to their memories of Egypt? (Hint: Look at the first and second phrases of the verse.)

God reminded them of what Egypt really represented—His faithfulness, His covenant, and His presence.

Look back at the painful words on your negative association chart. Can you look at that event or situation through the lens of Haggai 2:5 and rebrand your Egypt?

In the following chart, write your painful words again. Then, in the next column, write new meanings for those words based on God's faithfulness, His promises, and His presence.

WORD	REBRAND

When I did this exercise, I wrote the name of the city that represents stress and fear. Then I followed it with the redeemed rebrand of that weekend.

God PROMISED He would never leave me or neglect me, and He didn't.

God's PRESENCE was with me, and He provided a woman to help me.

God's PROTECTION guarded me and kept me safe. I can only imagine the potential dangers and harm He kept me from.

Now when I think of that city, it's rebranded as *safe*, *cared for*, and *victorious*.

I'm sure many of you listed words far more painful and traumatic than mine. You may have endured abuse, neglect, or injustice—events so painful that a simple chart won't give you a rebrand. I get it. I'm so sorry for your pain. Perhaps this chart can be a launching pad to healing. However, if it is too painful, don't do it. You may need to get with a Bible study buddy to talk and pray together. Your situation may be so painful you need to take courage and call a professional Christian counselor who can help you work through it. Depending on your situation, you may even need to contact the authorities.

Whatever the circumstances, my sister, the faithful promise of God is still true for you. He is with you, and, even now, He is stirring you to do the next right thing for your healing. Be brave and do it.

Now, let's look at the second phrase in Haggai 2:5. It hints at what God's covenant was. Write out the phrase again:

God assured the Jews that His Spirit remained with them.

Many Bible scholars think that the end of Haggai 2:4 and verse 5 are one thought.[9] Read them that way. What did God declare both before and after He mentioned Egypt?

"I am with you," declares the Lord Almighty . . .
my Spirit remains among you.
HAGGAI 2:4b,5b, NIV

Why do you think God said the same thing twice?

Sometimes we need to remember the truth that God is with us before our Egypt, that He is with us in our Egypt, and that He remains with us after Egypt. Pain doesn't change God's promise of His presence. Hard circumstances don't alter His covenant of faithfulness toward us.

Egypt wasn't the end of the Jews' story. God's faithfulness was.

Egypt—whatever yours may be—isn't the end of your story, either. God's faithfulness is.

To be stuck in the old brand of Egypt keeps you from the blessing you can have from the redeemed rebrand.

So take courage my sister. Get to rebranding! If we never let God's truth rebrand our past, we will live in constant discouragement and fear.

Fear is in the third phrase of this verse, so that's what we'll talk about tomorrow. Until then, I'm praying for you. May God give you comfort and clarity as you rebrand your Egypt with His faithfulness and truth.

Good job today!

DO NOT FEAR

We're almost finished with this session of study! Way to go!

Let's review. In order to be women who act with courage . . .

- We will avoid the comparison trap. Check.
- We're going to do our one thing. Check.
- We're going to live stirred up. Check.
- We're going to rebrand our Egypt. Check.

And today, we're going to do what God says: "do not fear" (Hag. 2:5).

Go ahead and read Haggai 2:1-5 to refresh your memory one more time.

Lord, please be our Teacher. Amen.

In Haggai 2:5 God reminded the weepy Jews that His promise still stood—His Spirit was with them; therefore, they had no reason to fear.

Yesterday, you asked questions about the first phrase of Haggai 2:5. What kind of questions come to mind about the last phrase—about God's Spirit remaining with them and the command to not fear?

I wonder, why didn't God say: *Do not quit,* or *Do not be discouraged.* Why didn't He instruct the Jews not to cry or not to give up? I mean, that's what they were doing. Or at least, that's what they were fighting against.

Of all the things God could have told them, why do you think God told them not to be afraid?

Do you struggle with fear? I sure do. I think we all do to some degree. That's normal. But let's be clear about what fear is so we can know how to follow the command God gives.

We all experience instant fear sometimes. When danger arises or something unsettles or startles us, we feel the emotion of fear. Our hearts race; we feel anxious, and we respond with fight or flight.

Yet there is another kind of fear. It's an everyday kind of fear based on our expectations and perceptions. For instance, we may fear rejection, which causes us to be over-the-top people pleasers. Or perhaps we hang on to a hefty fear of failure that shows up as perfectionism. This kind of fear also produces procrastination, isolation, tension, and being overly controlling. Oh, girl, this fear wears many masks! It's a response to the uncertainty of future outcomes, the unknown, and our lack of control.

Anything sound familiar here?

Fear can also be conditioned; it can become a habit. Sometimes, fear keeps us safe, but often, fear keeps us stuck in dysfunction and discouragement. It can paralyze us. Perhaps that's why God tells us not to fear. Fear is usually at the root of many unproductive and destructive emotions and actions.

As you think about that last paragraph, pause here for a brief lesson in the art of being human.

There are lots of emotions, right? Happy, sad, mad—we know the drill. Been there, felt them all. (And that was just before breakfast!)

In their book, *Life Lessons: Two Experts on Death and Dying Teach Us About the Mysteries of Life and Living,* Elisabeth Kübler-Ross and David Kessler contend that deep down in our cores, there are only two emotions: love and fear. The authors explain how all positive emotions come from love, and all negative emotions come from fear. From love flows happiness, contentment, peace, and joy. From fear comes anger, hate, anxiety, and guilt.

They wrote, "It's true that there are only two primary emotions, love and fear, but it's more accurate to say that there is only love *or* fear, for we cannot feel these two emotions together, at exactly the same time. They're opposites. If we're in fear, we are not in a place of love. When we're in a place of love, we cannot be in a place of fear. . . . It's impossible."[10]

Girl, the Bible said this long before Kübler-Ross and Kessler figured it out.

What does 1 John 4:8,16 say about Who God is?

What does 1 John 4:18 say about love and fear coexisting?

God is love. There is no fear in love. Perfect love casts out all fear. Where there is God, there is no fear. Love and fear cannot coexist.

How does that truth impact you? What does it mean in your daily life?

Can you really overcome fear with faith? Yes, you can! Learn how on the very first episode of my *4:13 Podcast* at **413podcast.com/01**. And the beauty of a podcast is that you can listen anytime.

In Haggai 2:5 God was basically saying to the Jews: *I was with you way back in the wilderness, and I am with you now. My Spirit is with you. Where I am there is love, and where there is love, there is no fear.*

Back to the art of being human—how do we live without fear when fear is a feeling and a hard-to-break habit? Sure, God's presence should be the antidote for fear, yet what does this look like in our real lives when opposition rises, disappointment grows, discouragement spikes, hope fades, and weariness sets in? How can we really be women who do not fear?

Take a moment to consider and pray about this. Ask God to help you understand. Talk about it with your Bible study buddies. I'll give you my thoughts as we wind up this week.

TWO WAYS TO BE A DO-NOT-FEAR WOMAN

1. **Practice God's Presence.** In Haggai 2 God reassured His people that His Spirit remained with them, and He promises us that He won't ever leave us either (Matt. 28:20; Heb. 13:5-6). But sometimes, we need to hone in on that truth. We need to practice God's presence like Brother Lawrence. Have you heard of him?

Brother Lawrence was a French lay monk who lived in the seventeenth century. He worked in the monastery kitchen where his love for God grew and his awareness of

God's presence became a practice. He wrote, "We can do *little* things for GOD; I turn the cake that is frying on the pan for love of Him, and that done, if there is nothing else to call me, I prostrate myself in worship before Him, Who has given me grace to work; afterwards I rise happier than a king. It is enough for me to pick up but a straw from the ground for the love of GOD."[11]

Don't you love that?! Every little thing Brother Lawrence did, he did for God. That level of love and commitment brought him a greater awareness of God's constant presence. He also wrote, "I make it my business only to persevere in His holy presence, wherein I keep myself by a simple attention, and a general fond regard to GOD, which I may call an *actual presence* of GOD; or, to speak better, an habitual, silent and secret conversation of the soul with GOD."[12]

Sister, we can have that same silent, secret conversation of the soul with God no matter where we are or what we're doing. We can tune into His presence because He is with us, in us, for us, and beside us. What we do, we do for the love of God. Wherever we are, we are in the presence of God.

So if fear plagues you, begin to practice God's presence.

I will practice the presence of God by . . .

2. **Do Something.** It is no coincidence that God told His people in Haggai 2:4 to get back to work in the midst of commanding them not to be afraid.

Earl Miller, a neuroscience professor at MIT, found that humans cannot focus on more than one thing at a time. His research has shown that "since our brains only can consciously focus on one thing at a time, once you are in the act of doing, your fear fades away. Therefore, taking action reduces conscious fear."[13]

Don't you love that? Even planning, making a commitment to do something, will reduce your fear because your brain will be focused on something other than the fear.

With God's presence and a plan, you're on the road to being a do-not-fear woman! So if fear is dogging you, what will you now do to combat that?

I will . . .

My friend, often when we read words from Scripture that are to-the-point imperatives, such as "do not fear," they can sound like a drill sergeant barking a command. But the more I read, "do not fear" in this context, it seems to be more a comfort than a command. Think about it. God, who is full of compassion, reassures His people: Don't fear; don't be afraid; I am here. I have been with you from the beginning, and I am sticking around. I won't leave. So when you hear the command of God to not be afraid, receive it as comfort, assurance, and peace. Pause and ponder this. Put down your pen and sit with your Father God. Practice His presence right now and receive His comfort.

He is with you my sweet sister, so take courage!

Session Four is a wrap! You did it! Yay, you! I'm so proud of you! We're in this together.

Love,

Jennifer

Notes

Group session 5

Welcome and Prayer

VIDEO NOTES

_____ is not one and done.

Discouragement is _____, but it's not real estate.

When you live in the _____ of God, you live out the _____ of God for your life.

Hannah is the _____ _____ version of *Anna.*

Hannah and *Anna* mean "_____" and "_____."[1]

The discouragement in your life may be the very thing that God is using to position you to _____ _____ more _____.

Three Courage Confessions

1. It is what it _____.

    • _____ women learn to look at the reality that God has allowed them to experience and say, "OK. It is what it is."

2. I _____ more than I see.

    • The world desperately _____ what God has wired you to do.

3. I am never _____.

    • When you feel the most alone, abandoned, or discouraged, that is when you are the _____ alone because God is near to the _____.

Would you like to read my written summary of this video teaching? Just go to *jenniferrothschild.com/takecourage*

CONVERSATION GUIDE

Video 5

DAY 1: What is the comparison trap and how can it hinder your spiritual life?
How can seeing things through the lens of what God can accomplish help you get out of the comparison trap?

DAY 2: How has God spiritually gifted and shaped you for ministry?
How are you using your giftedness to honor the Lord and serve the church?

DAY 3: Is there something in the past you tried to do for God in your strength alone?
How did that work out for you? Why are we so prone to try and accomplish things in our own power?
How can we live stirred up by God's Spirit on a daily basis?

DAY 4: What words trigger a negative emotion or memory for you? What words do the same in a positive way?
How can you rebrand those negative words to see them through God's perspective?

DAY 5: Do you struggle with fear? How does fear paralyze us spiritually?
How can you practice God's presence and take action to combat the fear you experience?

 **To access the video teaching sessions, use the instructions in the back of your Bible study book.**

The Affirmation of Faithfulness

Day 1

SHAKEN AND UNSHAKEABLE

Hey, sister! Pull up a chair. Welcome to Session Five! This week we're going to get a handle on why we can take courage. We're now halfway through Haggai's second sermon. But since it's been a while since we started this thing, pour your coffee or tea and sit back to read all of Haggai again to refresh your memory and keep your context. It's only thirty-eight verses, so you'll finish it before your mug is empty!

(In fact, my favorite app, Dwell, can read it to you in eight minutes, forty-two seconds! If you want to check it out, go to JenniferRothschild.com/Dwell).

Now that you've read it, let's begin by praying Psalm 86:11.

Write it out here as you pray it:

God, please teach us. We want to walk in Your truth. Amen.

OK, here we go. We're smack dab in the middle of Haggai's second sermon in chapter 2, verse 6. As you read the verse, answer the following:

Who is speaking?

What is going to happen?

When is it going to happen?

There's going to be a whole lot of shaking going on—in a little while.

How do you feel about those words, "in a little while" (CSB)? Well, if I ask my son to take out the trash and he answers, "In a little while," I don't feel so good about that!

To help you answer, imagine this . . .
If you call your dentist with a ginormous toothache, and he tells you to come in, and he will see you in "a little while," how would you feel? Hopeful? Anxious? Assured? Insecure? Irritated? All of the above?! "In a little while" is vague, isn't it? It could mean ten minutes or ten years!

But suppose you've been going to your dentist for twenty years. He's always been on time with your appointments, has never left you waiting, and has always gotten you in the chair on time. If he said, "Come on in, I'll see you in a little while," you would probably feel hopeful because you know how he manages time. He wouldn't make that promise just to have you throb miserably in his waiting room for hours while you endure endless tracks of Kenny G as fish lazily swim past you in the tank. That wouldn't fit who he is, right?

Our feelings about the words "in a little while" are directly connected to who says those words. So, when we hear God say "in a little while," we need to hear it based on who He is and how He manages and perceives time.

> Do a search in your favorite Bible resource for *time*. Jot down some of the references you find and then summarize God's perspective of time based on those verses. (Hint: Search for more than the word *time*. Look for words that indicate time, like *year, hour, day,* or *pass*.)

> **Scripture Starters**
> Job 14:2 • Psalm 90:4 • Psalm 144:4 • Luke 21:33 • 2 Peter 3:8

> Based on these verses, summarize how God perceives or operates in time:

I think Peter summed it up best in 2 Peter 3:8. He reminded the antsy church who was wondering if Christ would keep His promise to return that God's view of time is nothing like ours. God is eternal. He is transcendent, existing outside of space and time. He declares "the end from the beginning" (Isa. 46:10). We, on the other hand, are finite, limited by time and space. Our lives are short, like a breath, a passing shadow. We feel the quick passage and urgency of time.

The rebuilding Jews in Haggai's day probably wrestled with the notion of time, too. It took time to finish the temple. They used their time to update their paneled houses. They may have felt there wasn't enough time or that time was moving too fast. But when they heard the words "in a little while," they heard them from the mouth of a prophet representing the voice of God.

Prophets took the long perspective. They spoke of the time-bound things in relation to eternity. In this way, they used a constant foreshortening. So, even if it took a long while in light of eternity, it was a little while! The rebuilding Jews may not have known if "a little while" meant ten minutes or ten thousand years, but they knew it would happen.

> Look again at 2 Peter 3:8-9.

> What does this passage say about God's timing in keeping His word?

> He's not slow about it. He doesn't delay in keeping His word. What do you think the phrase "as some understand slowness" (NIV) or "as some understand delay" (CSB) in verse 9 means?

What might seem to us as God dragging His feet about a promise is actually a reflection of His patience and plan. We need to keep this in mind so we don't get discouraged or impatient with His patience, especially when we find ourselves in the midst of a long obedience or when we've grown weary from doing good, of building or rebuilding.

> Rewrite Galatians 6:9 as a declaration, an "I will" kind of statement, to affirm that you will trust God's timing and not give up or give in.

That's you, sister! You won't grow weary in doing your thing even when you're worn out. But let's be honest, some fruit takes a long time to grow and show. It's possible you may not ever see the fruit of your faithfulness on this side of heaven. However, that doesn't mean the seeds you planted are not taking root. God sees your work, and He is faithful. We can get discouraged when "in a little while" takes a long while. But Galatians 6:9 reminds us there is and will be a "proper time" for all your diligence, obedience, perseverance, and faith to bear fruit.

Like me, you probably need to be reminded often of that truth. Chances are, a Christian sister around you probably needs the reminder. Pause and ask God who might need this encouragement. If someone comes to mind, text or call that person right now. If you're texting, snap a picture of the paragraph above and attach it. Tell your friend you were thinking of her when you wrote your declaration. (It's a Hebrew 3:13 way to live!)

Now, there were two words I intentionally overlooked in Haggai 2:6: "once more." Those two little words probably gave a clue to the Jews what "in a little while" could have meant.

What do you think those two little words indicated?

Yep, you got it. "Once more" indicated that a shaking had taken place earlier in history.

Can you think of another time when there was a whole lot of shaking going on? (Hint: Read Exodus 19:18.)

Shaking number one:

Moses consecrated the people and had them stand around Mount Sinai. Then God descended in fire, and the whole mountain shook. Following this event, God summoned Moses to the top of the mountain where He gave Moses the Law. Can you even imagine? Later, we'll discuss why there was such a shaking.

But for now, let's see how that original shaking compares to the one that will occur "in a little while."

Fast forward past the time of Haggai when another shaking occurred Check out Matthew 27:50-52 and note the event.

Shaking number two:

The Jews in Haggai's day knew that God descended and shook Mount Sinai before giving the Law to Moses. What they didn't know was that "in a little while," about five hundred years after they heard Haggai's message, God would descend in Christ. Jesus Himself said He came not to abolish the Law but to fulfill it (Matt. 5:17-18). When He completed His work on Mount Calvary, the world was shaken again. Thank You, Jesus!

Many scholars believe Haggai was also referring to another shaking still yet to come.[2] Find Isaiah 24:19-20, Matthew 24:29-30, and 2 Peter 3:10 and note what the third shaking may be.

Shaking number three:

Many believe this shaking will occur as part of the events surrounding Christ's return.[3] Exactly when the shaking will occur is debatable. For our learning here, it's not important, so we're not going to get hung up or distracted by the timeline. What we can know for certain is that "in a little while," there will be a day when God will shake this world up one final time.

As we close, let me give you two personal courage boosters from my heart to yours.

First, your personal world may feel shaken. Perhaps it's a financial difficulty, an illness, or somebody's bad choices. Whatever it is, you've been shaken to your core. I encourage you to hold on to Psalm 16:8, my friend. Keep your eyes on the Lord. When He is at your right hand, you will not be shaken. Meditate on Psalm 62 also and lean hard on your Rock. He's got you.

Second, you may be in a waiting season. You may feel weighed down with doubt or weariness, and your "little while" is taking way too long. My friend, listen and meditate on Psalm 27:14, "Wait for the LORD; be strong, and let your heart be courageous" (CSB). Wait for the Lord. His timing is perfect even when it doesn't seem perfect. As you wait on Him, your strength will be renewed, and, eventually, you will rise on wings like eagles (Isa. 40:31)!

Don't miss out on those two little words in Psalm 27:14: "take courage" (ESV). Yes, my sister, take courage for God is with you.

Well, my mug is empty, and my heart is full of hope. I pray you heard God's voice today. Good stuff. Thank You, Lord.

See you tomorrow.

 This week, as you dive into God's faithfulness, listen to the Session Five songs of my *Haggai* playlist at **jenniferrothschild.com/ takecourage**.

YOUR DEEPEST LONGINGS MET

Hello, lovely! As I sat down with my laptop and a steaming cup of jasmine tea, I listened to this verse, Haggai 2:7, over and over and realized I need some strong coffee instead of this dainty tea! Something quite unexpected is in this verse. As we begin, pray and ask God to teach you.

"I will shake all the nations; and they will come with the wealth of all nations, and I will fill this house with glory," says the LORD of hosts.
HAGGAI 2:7, NASB

Let's break this verse into parts like we did with the verses last week. Write the three phrases found between the punctuation:

We examined the first phrase, "I will shake all the nations," yesterday. And we'll look at it again in our group time, so we won't spend any time with that phrase today. All aboard! We're moving on to the next phrase, "and they will come with the wealth of all nations." Or, as the King James Version reads: "the desire of all nations shall come."

Have you ever heard the phrase, "desire of nations?" (Hint: Think mangers and mistletoe.) Yep! Verse four of "Hark! The Herald Angels Sing"—"Come, Desire of Nations, come! Fix in us Thy humble home."[4] Now you'll be humming it all day. Sorry!

Based on Charles Wesley's carol, what do you think the phrase "Desire of Nations" is referring to? Yes, Jesus, the Messiah. Please don't think me a Grinch® or a heretic, but based on the Hebrew and the context of the verse Wesley pulled his lyric from, that may not be the exact or best interpretation. Now, don't panic. This won't mess with Christmas or your theology.

Use your favorite Bible app to read Haggai 2:7 in several different versions. Jot down what other words are used instead of "desire of all nations."

The original Hebrew is *khemdah,* and it's a collective singular.[5] That means the idea the word expresses is plural. The Hebrew smarties believe the better way to translate this phrase in Haggai 2:7 is *what is desired* or *desired.*[6]

How does Haggai 2:8 support this interpretation? In this verse, what is desired?

The context and the original Hebrew suggest that the "desire of all nations" refers to wealth, treasure, precious, material things, the silver and gold.[7] In The Message, Eugene Peterson paraphrased it simply as, "They'll bring bushels of wealth."

The idea was that other nations would freely give their wealth and resources to help complete the work on the temple. And as verse 8 emphasizes, all the treasures of the earth already belong to the Lord and are His to use as He sees fit.[8]

While Wesley's use of "Desire of Nations" might not be the best scholarly interpretation, it was the traditional view held by many people, including some ancient Jewish rabbis, early Christian leaders, even many modern commentators.[9] With that in mind, let's consider for a moment how the "desire of all nations" reference to Jesus can still apply.

What do we as humans ultimately treasure and long for? How does that relate to or represent the Messiah? Jot down your thoughts.

Sometimes examining what we treasure and desire gives us a chance to discern what we truly long for. The earthly things we seek are a hint that our hearts, our very natures, deeply long to be satisfied.

Since God made us for Himself, ultimately our greatest desire is for Him. As the writer of Ecclesiates said, God has "set eternity in the human heart" (Eccl. 3:11, NIV). But we easily get distracted and settle for less. Kind of like the Jews in Haggai focused on their paneled houses instead of God's house. Paneled houses, status, wealth, security, anything else is a shadowy substitute for what we find in Christ. Don't get me wrong, though. Desires are good things when our delight is in God. We can enjoy the beauty of nature, the artistry of the symphony, the joy of a relationship, and the security of shelter.

C. S. Lewis illustrates this so perfectly in his sermon, *The Weight of Glory*. (If you know me, you know I couldn't pass up an opportunity to quote my favorite dead author!)

"The books or the music in which we thought the beauty was located will betray us if we trust to them; it was not *in* them, it only came *through* them, and what came through them was longing. These things—the beauty, the memory of our own past—are good images of what we really desire; but if they are mistaken for the thing itself, they turn into dumb idols, breaking the hearts of their worshippers. For they are not the thing itself; they are only the scent of a flower we have not found, the echo of a tune we have not heard, news from a country we have not visited."[10]

Don't you love that? If we or nations mistake the wealth, treasure, or whatever is desired, "for the thing itself, they turn into dumb idols, breaking the hearts of their worshippers."

Sometimes when we find ourselves discouraged and ready to throw in the towel, it's because our desires are misplaced or misunderstood—we've settled for "dumb idols."

> How does this hit you? Have you settled for some dumb idols? Have you "planted much, but harvested little"? Do you "eat, but never have enough"? Do you "drink, but never have your fill"? Do you earn wages, "only to put them in a purse with holes in it" (Hag. 1:6-7, NIV)?

> If so, ask God to help you name the dumb idols and give you courage to renounce them and put them back into their proper place in your heart.

> Dear God,
> My dumb idols are . . .

> Help me . . .

> Amen.

C. S. Lewis also wrote, "Creatures are not born with desires unless satisfaction for those desires exists."[11] God created you with desire because He is the fulfillment of desire.

Use Psalm 38:9 to guide you into honest confession to God about your desires and longings.

Use Psalm 10:17 to guide you into praise and assurance as you lay your longings before Him.

Use Psalm 73:26 to guide you into a prayer or declaration about your deepest desire being met.

Charles Wesley might not have drawn from the most precise scholarly interpretation of Haggai 2:7, but, sister, who am I to say he got it wrong? Jesus, the ultimate Desire of Nations did come to make a way for us to have our deepest longings met through a relationship with Him. And He is coming again that we might experience satisfaction in Him for eternity.

Whew! Beautiful!

Fa la la la la, la la la la!

Today's thoughts could have been a little heady. What matters most is not that our heads are smarter, but that our hearts are changed. As you finish up today's session, go to your favorite music source and listen to "Yearn" by Shane & Shane. Ask God to make that your prayer, too—that He would be your greatest desire.

Oh, Lord, may we note the fragrance of that unfound flower; may we tune our hearts to the beautiful strains yet unheard, and may we feel the most satisfying ache of longing as our truest desire is for You and found in You alone. Amen.

Day 3

FILLED UP

It's before dawn, and I'm sitting at my table by the big kitchen window. Pull up a chair. I want you to experience this with me. There's an orchestra of crickets and full-throated mourning doves regaling me from my backyard. The water fountain I gave Phil for Father's Day is gurgling and babbling like a million little giggles on my deck. It won't be long before a puddle of sunshine is on the floor by the window. I don't have to see it; I can feel it when it warms me. The air is thick with the fragrance of coffee, and, as I breathe it in, every knot in my shoulders loosens a bit.

The cup of dark roast I hold steams my face and warms my hands. I realize how my senses are filled up with the richness of life. I open up Haggai to the verse we are studying today.

Go ahead and open your Bible and find it, too—Haggai 2:7. We're focusing on the last phrase. Isn't that a beautiful Scripture to read as we spend time with our Father God and His Word today?

> Pause and be present where you are. Listen to what surrounds you. See what is before you. Note the beauty, the wonder, the good stuff. What is filling your house or space? Describe where you are and what you feel, see, smell, and hear. What is filling your senses?

Lord, make us present here where we are. Thank You, Lord, that this Word is for us today. Teach us what this Scripture means and how we can apply it today, in Jesus' name. Amen.

> Before we dig in, read Haggai 2:1-7 again in your Bible so you remember the context. (I know you've slept since we last studied this verse.)

> Now, back to the last phrase in Haggai 2:7. What did God say He would do in His house?

What do you think it means for God to fill His house with His glory?

Haggai may have been standing by the construction site of the temple when he preached these words. He may have pointed to the foundation and the altar when he proclaimed "the word of the LORD" (Hag. 2:1).

If you were one of the Jews listening to Haggai's second sermon, what would you have thought? How do you think you might have felt when you heard Haggai's words?

There's no right or wrong answer here, by the way. I wonder if I were standing there, gazing at a temple I knew was going to be smaller and less grand than Solomon's, would I have felt a tad skeptical: *Really? God's going to fill THIS house with glory? This itty-bitty thing?*

Haggai's hearers, especially those who had seen Solomon's temple, probably thought about how Solomon's temple was filled with God's glory.

Pause here and read 1 Kings 8:10-11 and 2 Chronicles 5:13-14.

Describe what took place:

 Do you have a hard time believing your story can reflect God's glory? Listen in on my podcast conversation with Jackie Hill Perry as she shares how God's hand is over all our stories—for His glory! Go to 413podcast.com/83 to listen.

Amazing, right? Perhaps the people thought nothing could top that experience. But something doesn't have to be grand to be filled with glory. Sister, that is a radical statement. That means God's glory can permeate every chapter of your story.

You know why? Find 1 Corinthians 6:19-20 and describe who or what you are according to these verses:

I am . . .

Yes! You are now the temple of the Holy Spirit!

What does Ephesians 3:19 say is the result of knowing the love of God?

I am . . .

What does 2 Corinthians 3:17-18 say about God's glory?

I _____ _____ His glory.

I am . . .

According to 2 Corinthians 4:7, you are a jar of clay that holds a treasure. What does 2 Corinthians 4:6 say the treasure is?

Girl, you need to pause and read all that out loud! That is some radical truth about you. You are God's valued temple, the dwelling place of His Holy Spirit.

You are filled with all the fullness of God. You behold (or reflect) His glory, and you are being changed to be like Him with ever-increasing glory.

And, as a jar of clay, you hold within you "the Light of the knowledge of the glory of God in the face of Christ" (2 Cor. 4:6, NASB).

Girl, that means when we are filled with Jesus, we are filled with glory!

Sounds simple, right? Then why is it that I'm not always sure how to live it? I mean, let's face it, it's pretty radical that God calls us His temple. To think that His glory can fill our temples—our messy, frazzled, mundane, beautiful, and normal lives—blows me away.

So how do we really live "filled with His glory" in our ordinary lives in an everyday sort of way? Begin with an empty cup.

Similar to me pouring coffee into my empty mug, God pours Himself into our yielded lives. But here's the thing: Sister, if I leave the dregs from yesterday's coffee in my cup, I couldn't fill it with fresh-brewed goodness this morning. We need to show up empty in His presence, ready for Him to fill us. We need to empty our hearts of past sin. We confess it, repent, and ask God for forgiveness. We pour out our hearts before Him, admitting our need for Him.

We are emptied of self and filled with His fullness. His peace becomes our peace. His power infuses our strength. His truth informs our perspective. His glory becomes what grounds us and shines through us.

As you pour your morning coffee, tea, juice, or Diet Coke®, pray "Lord, I lift my cup, please fill it up." Seriously! Make this a tangible example. Associate your spiritual needs with your physical needs, and it will be easier to keep your faith front and center of your life.

To live filled up, we consistently empty ourselves of our sin and self-sufficiency, then ask God to fill us through His presence and His Word and fulfill His will in us.

Here are three Psalms you can pray as you "lift your cup!"

Create in me a clean heart, O God, and renew a right spirit within me.
Psalm 51:10, ESV

My flesh and my heart may fail, but God is the strength of my heart and my portion forever.
Psalm 73:26, ESV

To You, O LORD, I lift up my soul.
Psalm 25:1, NASB

Lord, thank You that You have made us to be Your temple. May we walk worthy of our callings. We empty ourselves before You and ask You to fill us with Your glory. Amen.

Well, that gives us a lot to think about! Thanks for studying your heart right along with the Scripture. May we all keep knowing and growing.

See you tomorrow!

Day 4

A GREATER GLORY

Hey there! After spending time thinking about God's glory in Solomon's temple yesterday, I couldn't get it out of my mind. Can you even imagine how heart-stopping, jaw-dropping, and life-altering it must have been to witness God's glory filling the temple? Well, that same kind of heart-stopping, jaw-dropping, and life-altering reality is ours to experience every single day because we are now God's temples. He lives in us through the presence of the Holy Spirit. God's glory is in us.

Wow.

Before we open the Word, let's humble our hearts before our great God. Thank Him for sending His Holy Spirit to dwell in you. Ask Him to be glorified in you, His temple, in all you do and say.

Dear God,

Amen.

Now, read Haggai 2:1-9. Then, reread and reflect on verses 8 and 9 because that's where we'll focus our study today.

Rephrase what God said in verse 8 without using the words *silver and gold*.

What do you think silver and gold represented to the Jews?

These were folks who wept at the foundation of the temple because it was so puny. They knew they didn't have silver or gold to adorn it and make it like Solomon's temple. Silver and gold could have represented provision or wealth to the Jews, or maybe it was a symbol of their glorious past. Just five verses earlier, they were wiping their tears and digging themselves out of the comparison pit, remember?

What do you think was the point of God saying the silver and gold were His? Before you answer, glance back at Haggai 2:1-7 for context and then circle the word below that best applies.

Reprimanding • Reassuring • Reiterating • Rebuking

Why did you circle that word?

Here's my take on it. These people didn't have the wealth to adorn the temple with silver and gold. In fact, their disobedience and misplaced priorities had landed them in the poor house. But God told them not to fear, reiterating He was with them and reminding them that the silver and gold were His anyway. In other words, God was saying, "I've got this!"

While some might see this as a rebuke, I think it was more a reassurance, another example of God's mercy for His people.

Pretend you're standing with the Jews just after Haggai had spoken these words of the Lord. Rephrase Psalm 50:10-12 into a confession of truth and affirmation that you could share with the Jews.

Do you need to preach that truth to yourself today? If so, explain why. Then, rephrase those verses once again with your name in it.

Don't forget, sister, God owns it all. That's why you can take courage. He is the One who supplies your needs (Phil. 4:19) and in Him you lack nothing (Ps. 23:1).

Because the Jews were probably thinking of the splendor of Solomon's temple and their inability to outfit the new temple in the same way, God reminded them that He would supply what was needed. He would shake the nations, and their treasures of gold and silver (which God Himself actually already owned) would adorn the new temple. However, God made clear that the physical beauty of the place wasn't to be the source of its splendor. You must understand verse 8 in light of verse 9.

> What do you think was the main idea God was presenting in Haggai 2:9?

When God said the future temple would have greater glory, He wasn't talking about an abundance of precious metals. In fact, the physical beauty of Solomon's temple wasn't what made it glorious. The glory came from God's presence.

> In Haggai 2:9 Haggai relayed God's own words, saying the final glory of this house would be greater than the first. What do you think God meant?

> Some scholars believe this house with greater glory was referring to the temple described in Ezekiel 40–43.[12] Pause here and take a few minutes to read those chapters and see what you think.

Earlier in his book, Ezekiel described how the glory of the Lord left the temple. This happened before the temple was destroyed in 586 BC. (See Ezek. 10:1-4,18-19; 11:22-23.) This would have been devastating to the Jewish people. They falsely believed that God could and would never leave His temple. For that reason, the people thought they were safe from their enemies (Jer. 7:4). So they ignored Jeremiah's and Ezekiel's warnings of God's judgment if they didn't repent. You know the rest of that sorry story.

The Jews in exile knew God's glory had abandoned the temple. But God had not abandoned His people. Just like Jeremiah, Ezekiel encouraged the exiles by telling them they wouldn't be stuck in the past. A future glory was to come. And, by the way, my sister, that truth is for you also. God has not and will not abandon you, and you are not stuck in your past either. Your "light and momentary troubles" are achieving for you an eternal glory that far exceeds them all (2 Cor. 4:17, NIV).

God gave Ezekiel a vision of the future glory of the temple (Ezek. 40–42). But the most encouraging words came in Ezekiel 43.

> Read Ezekiel 43:1-7.
>
> Describe what was happening in these verses. Put yourself there. Use first-person language, as if you are seeing it, feeling it, and reporting it.

Wow! What a scene, right?

Now, pause for a bit of clarification here. Scholars debate how Ezekiel's vision should be interpreted. Some believe Ezekiel was describing a literal event where a more glorious temple will be constructed in the millennial kingdom. Other Bible smarties think the vision is figurative, representing God dwelling in all His glory with His people once again in a perfect relationship.[13]

But back to our guy Haggai. Regardless of how you interpret Ezekiel's prophecy, Haggai seemed to speak of more than just what would happen to the temple the people were rebuilding. It seems the "final glory" or "greater glory" isn't about structure or silver. It's about the Savior!

Haggai's "greater glory" pointed to the coming of the Messiah, Jesus.

> Read John 1:14. Use your favorite online resource to find the verse in as many versions as you can.
>
> List how Jesus' coming to earth is described:

Jesus, who is full of "glory as the one and only Son from the Father" (NIV), became flesh and dwelt among us, pitched His tent, made His home, moved into the neighborhood to tabernacle with us. That is the greatest glory imaginable!

He is with us now and will be with us forever.

Now, read Revelation 21:22.

What did John tell us about the final temple?

In the new Jerusalem, where all of us who know Christ will live forever, there will be no need for a physical temple "because the Lord God the Almighty and the Lamb are its temple" (CSB). See? It's not about the silver; it's all and always has been about the Savior.

Sister, this calls for a pause to ponder and praise. So put down your pen and lift your hands in gratefulness and celebration. Praise God, celebrating that He dwells in and with you. I'm doing it right along with you. Oh, thank You, Jesus!

No matter where you are in life, no matter what you may fear or how you may feel, you can take courage because God is with you. Ultimately, we look forward to the time when "'the tabernacle of God is among men, and He will dwell among them, and they shall be His people, and God Himself will be among them, and He will wipe away every tear from their eyes; and there will no longer be any death; there will no longer be any mourning, or crying, or pain; the first things have passed away'" (Rev. 21:3-4, NASB).

And all the sisters said, "Amen!"

THE PROMISE OF PEACE

Here we are on the last day of this week. Way to go, sister girl, for sticking with this!

Today, we're focusing on the promise found in the last phrase of Haggai 2:9. Before we start, pause and pray, asking God to open your heart to the truth He wants to show you through His Word.

Look again at Haggai 2:9.

What was the promise?

Deep breath. Breathe in, breathe out. Ahhh . . . peace. God promised peace.

Peace. We want it. We need it! But what is it exactly? (Big grin!)

If you are ambitious, check a lexicon to find the Hebrew word for *peace* in Haggai 2:9 and write it here. (Google® *Hebrew lexicon* with the reference and the word *peace* in quotes.)

If you'd rather me do it for you . . . spoiler alert . . . here it is!

The Hebrew word for *peace (shalom)* can also be translated as *completeness, soundness,* or *welfare.*[14] That's why Eugene Peterson paraphrased the promise as "wholeness and holiness" in *The Message.* Pour some coffee or tea and ponder this.

Journal how God has given you His peace in the form of completeness, soundness, and welfare.

God has given me completeness . . .

God has provided me soundness . . .

> ### GO DEEPER
> Have you ever used a lexicon? A biblical lexicon is a great study tool that gives you the meanings and uses for a specific word in its original language. It's a great way to get a more complete understanding of the use of a particular word you see in Scripture.

God has granted me welfare . . .

We have wholeness, soundness, and welfare from God because we have peace with God through Christ. Haggai was ultimately pointing to this. The promise of peace in verse 9 would have been really good news to the people of Haggai's day because they had some hostile neighbors that kept giving them grief. I bet they were worn out from the conflict and threats and just wanted a little less egg-throwing and a lot more *kumbaya!* But ultimately, this promise of peace foreshadowed the coming of Jesus.[15]

You may live with "hostile neighbors" and be longing for peace, just like our friends from Haggai. Girl, if that is you, I hope the conflict ends soon. The kind of peace that comes when war ends allows us to exhale and relax, for sure. But God wants more than that kind of peace for you. He wants you to have rest and wholeness now—in the hard middle of anything you face. That kind of peace only comes through Jesus.

God's Word confirms that truth.

According to Isaiah 9:6, what is your Messiah Jesus called?

He is the . . .

According to Ephesians 2:14-18, how is Jesus described?

He is my . . .

According to John 14:27, what does Jesus give you?

He gives me . . .

The Prince of Peace came into the world to be with you. He came to be your peace, and He gives you peace because He gives you Himself.

Let's do something different as we wind this day and week up. Let's spend a few minutes experiencing the peace of God.

Here are some options:

1. Light a candle, put on some soothing instrumental or worship music, and just sit with the Lord and let His peace wash over you. Just linger. Don't be in a hurry. Take a moment to read the "Peace Scripture Starters" I listed below if you want to. Meditate on them and let God's Word guide your thoughts.

Peace Scripture Starters
Psalm 29:11 • Isaiah 26:3 • John 14:27 • John 16:33 • Philippians 4:6-7

2. If you're in the studying mood, do a word search on *peace* and jot down what consoles you or comforts you in the verses you find. Allow what you learn to become a reality in your life that settles you as you go through your day.

> **PEACE PIC**
>
> Take a picture of a peaceful scene or write out a peace Scripture and share it on Instagram®. Tag me, @JennRothschild, using the #TakeCourageStudy hashtag, so I can enjoy the moment with you. (But remember, I can't see it! Ha! So describe it for me!) Your post will encourage your friends, too, as you prompt them toward peace in their own lives.

3. Text your people and let them know you are going on a phone fast for the rest of the day so you can experience less noise and more peace. Don't try to replace the digital clutter today with anything but Scripture, worship music, and/or prayer. Turn off the TV and podcasts and just be present with your Prince of Peace as you go through the rest of your day.

Well, girl, Session Five is a wrap. Good Job! Next week we'll finish up the study by working through Haggai's last two sermons. Until then, this is my prayer for you, my courageous friend:

"May the God of hope fill you with all joy and peace as you trust in him, so that you may overflow with hope by the power of the Holy Spirit" (Rom. 15:13, NIV). Amen!

Shalom,

Jennifer

Group session 6

BEFORE THE VIDEO

Welcome and Prayer

VIDEO NOTES

The Hebrew word for *glory* is *kaved* which means "_____."[1]

When God's glory comes down, your _____ may come up.

Isaiah's Issues

1. "Woe is _____."

It is healthy for us to have a _____ _____ of who we really are.

2. "I am _____."

The Hebrew word in Hosea 4:6 for _____ is the same as the word for *undone* in Isaiah 6:5.[2]

3. "I am a man of _____ lips."

When the glory falls and it shakes you up, it is to _____ and _____ you.

Would you like to read my written summary of this video teaching? Just go to jenniferrothschild.com/takecourage

DAY 1: When have you experienced a waiting season in your spiritual life? How did you endure, and what did God teach you during this time?

What are some ways you have seen God be faithful to His promises in your life?

DAY 2: Is knowing Jesus your greatest treasure and joy? If not, what is? If so, how does your life show evidence of that?

What "dumb idols" are you prone to settle for instead of totally following Jesus?

DAY 3: If we truly understand what it means to be the temple of the Holy Spirit, filled with the fullness of God, how should that change the way we live? How should that dictate the purpose and direction of our lives?

What seems to be the thing that most often keeps you from living filled up with the Lord? What actions or changes need to take place for you to live the abundant life in Christ?

DAY 4: Do you ever struggle in your spiritual life with the "if only" syndrome—*If only I could do . . .* or *If only I could give . . . then I'd really be useful to the Lord?* What "if only" do you struggle with?

How does knowing God has given us everything we need "for life and godliness" (2 Pet. 1:3, CSB) help us shed the weight of "if only"?

DAY 5: How would you explain the peace of God to someone who doesn't know Him? Are you currently experiencing the peace of God? If so, how is God's peace helping you through your current situation? If not, what seems to be blocking God's peace in your life?

To access the video teaching sessions, use the instructions in the back of your Bible study book.

The Attitudes of the Heart

AVOID THE STINK

Nice title for this day, huh? Can you even believe we have almost made it through thirty-eight verses in Haggai, and it's only taken us six sessions? Ha!

In our last session together, we hear Haggai preach his third sermon and take a look at his closing mini-message.

> Read Haggai 2:10 and do the math to determine how long it's been since the Jews listened to Haggai's last sermon.

It appears that Haggai preached this third sermon about two months after he finished his second one and about three months from the time the Jews started working on the temple. By our calendar, the date would be December 18, 520 BC.[3]

> Read Zechariah 1:1.

> What was one thing that happened between Haggai's second and third sermons?

Yep, about a month before Haggai's third sermon, Zechariah started preaching, too. We met him and got a taste of his message back in Session Two, Day Five.

> What was the point of Zechariah's message in 1:1-6? What was the result of his preaching?

THE POINT	THE RESULT

Zechariah reminded the Jews to not behave like their ancestors. He made it clear that their forefathers' disobedience and stubbornness landed them in exile. But the current group of Jews had the choice to return to God. The people responded to Zechariah's message with repentance.

At this point, the Jews were tag-teamed by Haggai and Zechariah. They received exhortation and encouragement from both. And they upped their game because of it. The Jews had been working on the temple for the last three months, but then God gave Haggai a new message to speak. If you're a vegetarian, buckle up!

> Pause and ask the Holy Spirit to guide you and be your teacher as you read Haggai 2:11-14.

See why I warned the vegetarians? I won't even ask you to summarize what you read. I was pretty confused and a little grossed out when I read it. One thing about it—it's a good lesson in food management!

So, next time you tuck the holiest meat I know, aka Chick-Fil-A®, in the fold of your garment, don't expect its virtue to spread to the McDonald's® fries you stashed in your pocket if they accidentally touch. Just sayin'!

Let me set up a framework, and we'll figure this out together.

> First, who is speaking according to the first part of Haggai 2:11?

Yeah, sister, this is God Himself. While this passage may seem a little odd to us, we can't take it lightly or make light of it. If this matters to God, it matters to us. We'll just step into the culture of the original hearers to understand it.

Secondly, Haggai 2:11-14 is a Q&A between Haggai and the priests about ceremonial law. But the content applies to all of us.

> Let's talk about the two questions that Haggai asked the priests.

Question Number One (v. 12)

Haggai asked:

Priests answered:

What do you think God, through Haggai, was communicating through this question and answer?

Question Number Two (v. 13)

Haggai asked:

Priests answered:

What do you think God, through Haggai, was communicating through this question and answer?

In the first question, God seemed to be emphasizing that ceremonial cleanness was nontransferable. But the second question seems to make the point that ceremonial uncleanness could spread very quickly! (If you want to understand the priests' context for these questions and answers, read Leviticus 22.)

Just in case the priests or anyone else who was eavesdropping missed the point, Haggai applied the lesson in Haggai 2:14. Read and summarize Haggai's conclusion below.

As far as God was concerned, everything the people touched became defiled.

Read Haggai 2:14 again.

How did the Lord address the Jewish people?

He called them "this people" and "this nation." Why do you think God addressed them in this way?

If you're a mom who has ever had a misbehaving child, you may have done something similar. You may have described your son or daughter as "this child," or in speaking to your husband about your child said, "this son of yours!" Right?

Why would you, as a mom, use language like that when the child is clearly yours? Explain.

Yeah, you get it. In those misbehaving moments you don't love your child less, but you sure can get exasperated with Junior's disobedience and naughty rebellion. This creates a sense of separation between you and your little angel.

That's similar to what's happening here in Haggai. The Jews have so separated themselves from God by their sinful condition that He didn't even call them His people and His nation.[4] Oh, sister, that's what sin does. It separates us. It creates disconnected discomfort. So if you're feeling a little distance between you and God today, follow the promise of

1 John 1:9. Confess your sin. Walk away from it and walk toward God instead. He will forgive you and restore the closeness you long for. He doesn't love you less because you sin. Rather, He loves you too much to let you stay there.

OK, back to the stinky-meat scenario. It is like God was calling the people an unclean collective, spreading their uncleanness everywhere. But how could that be? We just looked at the calendar and saw that the people had been busy on the temple. It seems they were being obedient. So what gives? Why was the nation defiled?

> What do you think God was referring to here?

Productive hands with impure hearts build nothing of value. Ouch!

The people were in such a sick, sinful condition that even though they may have been busy with a sacred task, the Lord was not pleased. God cares about obedience, yes, but not just outward obedience.

> Look at the following Scriptures and note what God focuses on and values most. Rephrase each verse into a first-person statement about you.
>
> 1 Samuel 16:7
>
>
>
> Psalm 51:6
>
>
>
> Hosea 6:6

Read the statements you just wrote and form them into a prayer to the Lord. Linger with these truths in prayer to help you better understand what God values and how He sees your heart and your actions.

God sees your heart and wants truth and purity in the deepest part of you. God desires faithful love and an acknowledgment of who He is more than anything else. We need to realize that religious activity does not equal a devoted heart. Spiritual busyness does not make up for lack of spiritual intimacy.

So what is the answer? We don't want to be hypocritical. We don't want to be women of empty obedience. God deserves our pure and wholehearted obedience. Let's ask God to show us in His Word.

Look in your concordance or favorite Bible online resource for Scriptures on purity. Search for words like *pure*, *truth*, and *clean* to get you started. I will include "Scripture Starters" below.

Scripture Starters
Psalm 24:4-5 • Psalm 51:10 • Matthew 5:8 • 2 Corinthians 7:1 • Hebrews 10:22 • 1 John 1:9-10

Once you find and read these verses, pretend you are the Jews' doctor who is going to help them move from unclean to clean. Write out a prescription for what they should do or stop doing and include the potential result of their actions if they follow this prescription.

Well done, Doc! But here's the thing—whatever you wrote for the Jews to help them move from unclean to clean is what you and I need, too. We can be so easily deceived about the reality of our sinfulness, especially when we are busy with the things of God, like doing Bible studies and serving in the church.

Find Proverbs 16:2 and spend some time meditating on it.

Ask God to "weigh" you right now. Ask Him to give you His perspective. Though sin may be weighing your heart down, God can forgive. Just repent and start fresh. Don't move on until you confess and experience His cleansing. Write down the date and your experience somewhere on this page to remember God's forgiveness and purifying cleansing. Refer back to it when the enemy tries to condemn and accuse you. We all need to walk wisely when it comes to our own sneaky hearts because the other part of this truth is that sin is transferable!

Now, this may seem a little odd if you're unfamiliar with Old Testament lingo and law, but put yourself in the Jews' shoes as you read Leviticus 22:4-6 and Numbers 19:11.

How would you summarize and personalize the principle communicated in those verses?

For me, to put it simply: sin is contagious!

Now let me be clear here. We don't transfer the guilt of our sinfulness to each other when we shake hands at church. And just because we hug at Bible study doesn't mean we've shared the germ of disobedience. (Thankfully!)

However, we can become tempted and tainted by the company we keep (or the shows we watch, the podcasts we listen to, the books we read). We can allow others' sinful choices to influence us toward disobedience. Bad company corrupts good morals (1 Cor. 15:33).

In the same way, if we walk around like Pigpen from Charlie Brown®, with a puffy black cloud of sin surrounding us, we can spread that yuck to everybody we meet.

When we have a stinky attitude, it's easy to influence others. When we're unkind or gossipy, it invites others to go low along with us. Our personal purity of heart not only honors God and gives our obedience greater significance, it can be an influence for good to all we encounter.

So where do these truths hit you? Sometimes I think we just need to pause and ponder.

Ask yourself:

Do I need to walk away from influences that tempt or taint me? If so, what or who and how?

Do I need to turn from my sin and turn toward God in repentance so I become an influence for good to all I encounter? If so, write out your prayer of repentance, including a plea for God's strength and a plan for purity.

Sister, through Christ's grace and strength, we can maintain pure motives and pure hearts not only for our sakes, but for God's glory and others' protection.

Also, let's constantly ask God for wisdom when it comes to who and what influences us and where we hang out. Sin is infectious, and we are not immune.

God sees the attitude of our hearts before He pays attention to the activity of our hands. Our hands can be doing the work, but if our hearts are not in it or are in it for the wrong reasons, it stinks.

So, sister, let's avoid the stink!

Now, go get some Chick-Fil-A® and enjoy your day!

 In our final week together, as you finish up your study time, listen to the Session Six songs of my *Haggai* playlist at **jenniferrothschild.com/takecourage**.

Day 2

MARK THIS DAY

Have you ever experienced a day that impacted you so deeply that it became a marker for you? If so, you could probably give me a "before-that-day" life summary and then an "after-that-day" life summary, and the two would be very different from each other.

Well, pour your coffee or tea, pull up a chair, and I'll tell you about one of my "marker" days. One day, back in my thirties, Phil and I were in Nashville visiting a record producer about a future project. (Yes, I used to sing for people. Now I just sing in the shower!) We went to dinner with him and, as usual, I got chicken. We had a great meal, great conversation, and then went to the studio after dinner to sit in on a recording session he was doing with some backup singers. I sat near him on the other side of the glass and could hear all the oohs and aahs of First Call, the group doing the backup recording.

And the longer I sat there, the worse I felt.

Cramps. Nausea. Then it hit! "Phil! Take me to the bathroom!" What followed is not something you want to read, so I'll leave it to your imagination. After my run to the restroom, I thought I'd feel better, but it was just the beginning. Phil and I quickly left the studio and went straight to our hotel. We were up all night with me being sicker than I ever had been before or since. We left early the next morning, trying to get home to Florida to my doctor. However, we only made it as far as an Atlanta hospital emergency room because I was so dehydrated.

The hospital that day was crammed with very needy people, so they placed me on a gurney in the hall with a plastic bracelet on my wrist and a bucket by my cot. It was so awful. I laid there for three hours. By the third hour, I realized I had fewer cramps. The violent output slowed down and then stopped as quickly as it had started.

At that point, Phil looked at the clock and noted that it was exactly twenty-four hours since we had arrived at the studio the night before. We had no money to pay for a hospital bill, so he snapped that bracelet off my wrist, grabbed my shoes, and we left the bucket behind! That is when I learned about the power of food poisoning. I marked that day, sister! Before that day, I ate chicken in any restaurant, from any cook, without a thought. After that day, I order omelets!

OK, you get the ugly picture. Of course, not all "marker" days involve food poisoning. Some are heartbreaking and tragic, while some are beautiful and precious. But what they all have in common is that the after is very different from the before.

What are some of your "marker" days?

Now, read Haggai 2:15-18. Ask God to guide you in His truth as we study the Jews' "marker" days. Amen.

Let's start with Haggai 2:15. Write out the first phrase of that verse.

God was telling His people to consider "this day" as a "marker" day—a day they were to do two things. First, they were to look back. Second, the Jews were to look forward (more on looking forward tomorrow when we examine verse 18).

On this present day, Haggai told the people to consider what it was like in those past days before they started rebuilding the temple. He was saying to the Jews, "Take a seat in the thinking chair! Think about those days of your distraction, discouragement, and disobedience."

Read Haggai 2:16.

Record what those days were like.

Sometimes you and I must take a seat in the thinking chair and look back.

Why is it important to look back at times when we have been discouraged and disobedient?

What does verse 15 tell us about the importance of remembering?

Sometimes we want to completely forget about our sinful past or wrong choices because it is too painful and fills us with regret and shame. But sometimes we need "marker" days to look back and remember. Not to wallow, but to stay mindful of how every choice matters. And sister, that look back can also serve as a reminder of God's goodness and help us grow in our love and knowledge of Him.

> Read Lamentations 3:19-25. Beside each verse number, personalize that verse to reflect a time in your past when you felt distracted, discouraged, or disobedient, then how the Lord showed His faithfulness to you.

19:

20:

21:

22:

23:

24:

25:

Remembering your difficult days might remind you of discouragement, but it can also bring you hope as you remember the greater truth: "The LORD is good to those whose hope is in him, to the one who seeks him" (Lam. 3:25, NIV).

So, my friend, let's keep seeking Him.

OK, let's finish up with Haggai 2:17. Circle the phrase below that best captures the gist of that verse.

- Severe weather destroyed the crops and caused the Jews to seek God.

- God let the Jews' crops be destroyed to teach them a lesson.

- The people lost their crops due to bad weather, praised God, and replanted.

- God caused bad weather to destroy the Jews' crops in order to get their attention, but they didn't return to Him.

MARK THIS DAY!
Begin a #MarkThisDay habit on Instagram® or Twitter®. When you learn something from Scripture, when you give thanks, when you trust God for something hard, or when you make a spiritual choice or commitment, mark the day! Whatever is bringing you closer to God or helping you grow, post it and include the hashtag #MarkThis Day. That way, when your Bible study buddies and I search the hashtag, we can be encouraged, too! Tag me @JennRothschild so I can be sure to like it!

Bad weather didn't just randomly happen because of the climate or season. God didn't let some mildew grow and some wind blow. In this situation, God actually caused something hard and destructive in the Jews' lives. He intended it. He determined it.

How does that truth make you feel?

God's mercy can feel severe at times. Yet, because God is love, His ways are loving even if they appear to show up in hail, mildew, or blasting winds.

Take some time right now to pray through this difficult truth. When our hearts are breaking, and we have more questions than answers, we only want the God who calms the storms, not the One who may cause them. Use the following Scriptures to guide your thoughts about God and your prayer to Him.

- Deuteronomy 32:4

- Psalm 18:30; 115:3

- Isaiah 43:1-3a; 55:8-9

Dear God,

Amen.

In Haggai's day, the pain had a purpose. God used the mildew, wind, and hail to draw His people back to Him and what He called them to do.

If you are in a confusing season or in a painful circumstance, let this day be a "marker" day for you. Sweet sister, trust God to use this difficulty to draw you to Him. He does not intentionally cause or send every single suffering in your life, but He does allow them, superintend them, and redeem them.

He will use these tough days as stepping stones to draw you closer to Him as you seek Him in every hard minute. They will only become stumbling blocks of discouragement if you choose for them to.

Take courage. Don't let the mildew, blasting winds, or hail be wasted in your life. Instead, may you see the face of God more clearly because of every hard thing you face. Lord, make it so.

Peace to you today, my friend. See you tomorrow!

Day 3

BE PATIENT WITH THE SEED

Hey there! I saved you a seat at my kitchen table. I just made my coffee and realized how perfectly this cup in my hands represents these verses today. How, you may wonder? Because it took its normal sixty seconds to brew. You see, when I first got this coffee machine, I thought that brew time was lightning fast! But today, as I waited for the last drop to fall, I grew impatient and annoyed because it was taking so long. Oh, brother!

We live by fast food and in fast forward, don't we? If Google® takes more than two seconds to return a thorough and accurate answer to my question, I think something must be wrong with my phone. It shouldn't be this slow! Our instant lifestyles cause us to quickly become impatient with things we once considered quick conveniences.

If we learn anything from our study of Haggai, it's that we should caution ourselves against expecting immediate gratification.

Immediate results are not the automatic fruit of obedience or evidence of God's blessing. I think the rebuilding Jews had figured this out by this point in the story. At least, that's what they were hearing from Haggai in chapter 2:18-19. Before we jump in, let's pause and pray for God's wisdom as we walk through this passage.

> Lord, You are our teacher. Please guide us into wisdom and truth and may we be doers of Your Word, not just hearers. Amen.

> Read Haggai 2:15-19 but focus on verses 18 and 19.

Verse 18 uses the phrase "this day" again, referencing the present day (v. 15). Haggai even further clarified that it was the present day by providing the date: the "twenty-fourth day of the ninth month" (v. 10). He then made a confusing reference: "the day that the foundation of the LORD's temple was laid" (v. 18). He used this reference to mark the day the Jews began to rebuild the temple after Haggai's first sermon, the "twenty-fourth day of the sixth month, in the second year of King Darius" (1:15). However, that's not the date the foundation was laid to the new temple. The exiles had completed that construction approximately eighteen years earlier when they first returned (Ezra 3:8-10). Perhaps the timeline problem is resolved by digging further into the Hebrew word *yasad*, which can mean *to lay a foundation*, or *to restore or repair*.[5] The latter meaning could refer to work done on an existing structure, thus not precluding earlier work done on the temple.

Another possibility is that Haggai was alluding to a possible dedication ceremony for the temple work that took place on that particular day.[6]

Verse 19 marks the change that would follow. What was it? (Hint: The answer is found at the end of the verse.)

God told the Jews that because they began to rebuild the temple with wholehearted obedience, because they began to restore worship, He would bless them.

But how does the promised blessing relate to the first part of verse 19? Which of the following statements best capture what is happening in the first part of verse 19?

- Their crops will no longer bear fruit.

- Their seeds will just sit in barns.

- Their crops have not flourished yet, but they will.

To me, it sounds like God was saying their blessing will be a slow-growing one. That is my opinion, but quite honestly, this portion of the verse is hard to interpret.

It may be that the seed wasn't in the barn but was instead in the ground. The point is, blessing was coming.[7] Soon, whatever they had planted would grow. Whatever they sowed would sprout. They will have plenty once again. They will live in abundance. But the evidence of God's promised blessing was not yet hanging on the vine. The fig, pomegranate, and olive trees had not yet produced. The people probably glanced around and thought back to previous failed harvests, even as Haggai was pronouncing God's blessing upon their land. What God said and what they saw didn't seem to match.

Yet.

How would you have felt if you had been part of the group noticing the promised blessing was still yet to be seen? Better yet, how do you feel when God's promise of blessing doesn't match up to your current circumstances?

We often believe that when God promises blessing, it will show up as quickly as a Google® search result or a cup of coffee from a Keurig®! That's when we need to be patient with the seed.

When a blessing takes a long time to show up, it gives us time to grow up.

Let me give you an example from my life. I remember reading the book *Love and Respect* by Dr. Emerson Eggerichs after Phil and I had been married many years. When I read it, I wished we had read it many years earlier—like on our honeymoon! The descriptions of the conflicts and frustrations on most every page in the book matched ours exactly. After reading the book, I decided to try what Dr. Eggerrichs suggested. His solutions were based on Scripture, and I knew God honored obedience. So I gave it my best shot! I began to show Phil respect in ways he would recognize, expecting our twenty years of dysfunction and miscommunication to evaporate overnight.

Wrong.

The seed was in the ground, but the blessing of obedience would take some time to grow. I had to say to myself what Haggai was saying to the people in these verses. The years of sin and selfishness that we had perfected were not going to be erased overnight. Just because I started doing the right thing didn't mean habits of wrong thinking or behaving suddenly translated into instant right-relating. I had to trust that seed of humility and right behavior to grow. And while it grew, I did, too. The process of patience matured me.

> What about you? Is there a "seed" you need to be patient with? Think about this for a moment. Then either write a prayer for patience for the seed to grow or journal your thoughts about where you are in the process.

As we grow in patience, we grow in faith. As we grow in faith, our capacity for patience grows. We are all in process. Take some time in the next few days to be honest with a Bible study buddy about the seed you need patience for. Let her know your circumstances so she can pray for you and stand with you in faith. We all need to encourage each other to be patient with the seeds in our lives.

You can be patient with the seed because God is faithful with the seed.

Well, sister, that's it for today. However, I want to leave you with some encouragement if patience is hard for you. May these Scriptures be water for your seed.

But as for you, be strong and do not give up,
for your work will be rewarded.
2 CHRONICLES 15:7, NIV

For the revelation awaits an appointed time; it speaks of
the end and will not prove false. Though it linger, wait
for it; it will certainly come and will not delay.
HABAKKUK 2:3, NIV

Jesus replied, "You do not realize now what I am
doing, but later you will understand."
JOHN 13:7, NIV

You need to persevere so that when you have done the
will of God, you will receive what he has promised.
HEBREWS 10:36, NIV

Great job today, sister girl!

Thank You, Lord, for Your truth.

Now I'm going to sprint over to the coffee machine, whip up a cup of java, do a speedy Google® search, and then jump in the car for some fast food! Kidding!

Day 4

BE A COURAGE GIVER

Ta-da! Sister, you made it to Haggai's fourth and last sermon! It's a short one, and it's all about anticipation.

> **Read Haggai 2:20-23.**
>
> When did Haggai preach this final message?

Yep. This is on the same day as the last sermon he preached. Evidently Haggai had more to say, so he gave the people a coffee break and then got right back to it.

It seems Haggai was adding final words to summarize what mattered most in all his sermons.

> What theme that you've already read in Haggai do you detect in these three verses? (Hint: Look back at Haggai 2:6-9.)

Haggai was once again boosting his hearers with the reassurance that their present circumstances weren't all there was. Ultimately, a better day was coming when the Messiah would reign and establish His kingdom.

> **Read Daniel 2:44 and 7:27.**
>
> Based on those verses, describe what might have come to the people's minds when Haggai gave this encouragement:
>
> Daniel 2:44
>
> Daniel 7:27

The Jewish people were smack dab in the middle of their destroyed kingdom, struggling through all their rebuilding issues. But Haggai reminded them a kingdom was coming that would never be destroyed. The Messiah's kingdom would be everlasting, and all the supposed greatness of any kingdom that did exist would be handed over to the holy people of the Most High. In Haggai 2:21-22 God affirmed that He would prove Himself supreme over nature, stronger than any army, more powerful than any government. Everything would shake, but God's promise would stand. Yes! Go ahead, shout a *hallelujah* here!

What encouraging truths! (You can find similar encouragement in Revelation 19–20.)

You know what I love about this passage? It affirms that we all need to be reminded of truth and constantly encouraged by it. If Haggai repeated this encouragement in thirty-eight verses, how much more do we need to repeat encouragement to others and hear encouragement repeated to us over and over and over? Sister, our lives can look like those barren orchards or that half-repaired temple. Our present can look way different than God's promise, and we can feel more defeat than determination, right?

We need encouragement because courage evaporates easily.

> What is the difference between encouragement and compliments? (Check your dictionary.)
>
> Encouragement is:
>
>
>
> Compliments are:

Compliments flatter us. They are words that praise us, commend us, or bring attention to us. Encouragement fuels us. Encouragement infuses us with support, confidence, and courage.

> Which do you think you need most in this life? Encouragement or compliments? Both? Explain.

Oh, girl, I need words and actions from others that boost my power instead of words that just offer praise. I need courage far more than I need compliments. (But there is nothing wrong with a "you-look-so-cute-in-those-sassy-boots" kind of compliment. We need that, too, every now and then!)

I learned about the power of encouragement from a guide dog I once had many years ago. His name was William. (I know, I know. His name sounds like it should belong to a U.S. president or your grandpa more than a dog. I got him prenamed.)

It was a steamy July day in central Florida. I had been at the "dog school" for about two weeks of training learning how to work with William. He and I were both getting pretty tired. So far, we had worked on walking together and learning each other's pace. I had learned how to give him the correct hand commands, and he knew exactly what I meant if I told him, "Busy, busy." (If you don't know what that means, well, it's bathroom talk, so I won't elaborate.)

So on this day, we were trudging down the sidewalk in Palmetto, Florida, for another training session. The whole class was out with our dogs navigating some busy downtown streets and sidewalks. But William and I weren't keeping up with the class. We weren't lost or distracted; we were just hot and tired! We lagged a little as William slowed down. I stopped and gave him water to make sure he was hydrated since the temp was well into the 90s. He gulped in some H_2O and was good to go . . . for a little while. But within a few minutes, he would slow down again.

I tried to cheer him on: "Good dog, William. You're a good boy!" In response to my praise, he would wag his tail but barely pick up his pace. Finally, I realized we were way behind our group, and we needed to walk faster. I could have gotten a step ahead of my slow-poke William and dragged him, but that kind of defeats the purpose of a guide dog. Ya think?!

Instead of just saying "Atta, boy," I reached down and patted him on the top of his head and said, "You can do this, William." To my surprise, he got a little snap to his step. I petted him a little more as we walked, and he picked up his pace. In fact, every time I reached down to pat him on the back or jostle his ears, he got a little more motivated. His ears began to flop as he broke into a gallop! The more I petted, the faster he walked. He needed more than compliments; he needed encouragement. He needed to be infused with courage.

"You're a good dog" was a lovely compliment to a pup who had no idea what I was saying, but placing my hand on his head encouraged him. It served to infuse enough courage in him to strut all the way to the front of the dog line!

Encouragement gives us courage.

Our English word *encourage* comes from the Old French word *encoragier* which means *to make strong or hearten.*[8]

Do you need another dose of courage? Come on over to the *4:13 Podcast* with me and learn how you can choose courage, even when you don't feel brave. Go to 413podcast.com/21 to listen.

That's what Haggai was doing in these verses. He was using the truth to make Zerubbabel and the people strong and to hearten them. He didn't just say, "Way to go laying those stones. You are such talented and stylish stone layers. If Chip and Joanna could only see this!" Nope, he didn't flatter; he fueled them with the assurance that God is who He says He is and will do what He says He will do.

I'll be honest about this, one of the awkward things about blindness is that when I run into you at the store, I can't tell you how cute you look in that top or how much I love your hair color or how amazing you look since you cut sugar out of your diet. (I will probably tell you how good you smell though! Ha!) But as awkward and as frustrating as that is, it has made me go deeper so that I can give something far greater than compliments. It has nudged me to give something that lasts longer and means far more: courage.

As we finish up today, I want you to pause, put down your pen, lean back, and let me serve you up a venti size cup of courage.

- God has given you all you need for life and godliness, so keep doing your thing because God has equipped you (2 Pet. 1:3).

- Don't give up for you are not of those who shrink back (Heb. 10:39). Keep believing no matter what!

- You are shining like a star in the universe as you forbear and don't grumble or complain (Phil. 2:14). Way to shine, sister!

- God will finish what He started in you because He is the One who began this work in you (Phil. 1:6).

- You can be strong even if you don't feel strong because God is with you wherever you go (Josh. 1:9). So take courage!

Well, sister, encouragement is powerful, isn't it? It heartens us when we're weak, emboldens us when we're frightened, and spurs us on when we're weary. Serve up a big cup of courage to somebody you meet today. You can tell her she looks cute in her jeans because I bet she does, but don't stop there. Do what Haggai did. Fuel her with truth. Don't stop at flattery. Encourage her with the truth of who her God is and who she is because of Him.

When we give specific, biblical encouragement to someone, it helps us grow more convinced of the power of God's Word to make us strong also.

God is with you and working in you, my friend, so take courage!

Tomorrow is our last day. 😥 I can't wait to spend it with you and our guy Haggai! We will finish strong together. Cheers!

Day 5

BUILD MORE THAN YOU SEE

Hey, sister! Gotta be candid right up front. I have rewritten this day of study so many times because I really want it to be meaningful to you. I keep imagining you sitting at my kitchen table with me, wondering what you need most on this last day of study together. We've covered so many concepts and learned so much from these thirty-eight verses in Haggai, haven't we?

My prayer is that God is embedding the truths we've learned deep into our hearts so we will continue to love them and live them.

Let's pray for that. Pause and ask God to write the truths you've learned deep in your heart. (If you have some extra time, flip back through the study and highlight some of the phrases, quotes, and statements that impacted you the most. This will be a great review. Plus, highlighting these impactful words will make it easy for you to spot them when you need encouragement. Also, you can easily Instagram® or tweet them to spread encouragement.)

Pour your coffee or tea for our last bit of Haggai. We will trust God's Spirit to give you exactly what you need today.

> Read Haggai 2:20-23, focusing on verse 23.

Sound familiar? Probably. We skimmed the concept of this verse on Day Four of Session One (pp. 23-27) when we were getting acquainted with the ABCs of Haggai. Turn back and refresh your memory because today I want to take this passage in a slightly different direction.

> Now that you reviewed the significance of Zerubbabel, glance back at the beginning of each sermon in Haggai. Jot down to whom God, through Haggai, was directing each message.
>
> Haggai 1:1
>
>
>
> Haggai 2:1-2

Haggai 2:10-11

Haggai 2:20-21

Look at all four of the message recipients listed. If this were *Sesame Street*®, a hairy puppet would start singing, "One of these things is not like the other!" Do you see which one it is and why?

Yep. The last message in the Book of Haggai was directed to one man. Just one. God, through Haggai, was speaking directly to Zerubbabel, the leader of His people. All the other messages included Joshua or the people or the priests, but Haggai's final message was a One-on-one with Zerubbabel.

Why do you think God spoke directly to him?

How do you think Zerubbabel may have felt after hearing this personalized mini-message?

Perhaps God spoke straight to Zerubbabel because Zerubbabel was the leader of God's people. Leaders bear great responsibility. And, usually, the greater the responsibility a person has, the greater discouragement he or she may feel. Perhaps Zerubbabel felt encouraged and esteemed by God's One-on-one.

Since God narrowed down His message to one person, let's take it personally too.

Look one more time at Haggai 2:23 and note how personal it can be to you. What are the three names God calls Zerubbabel? (Hint: they all start with *S*.)

GO DEEPER

Your pastor needs your encouragement. All leaders question their abilities and value at times. Moses felt he wasn't gifted enough. Jeremiah questioned if he was too young. Gideon thought he didn't have the pedigree. I guarantee that your pastor feels much like those biblical men on some days. All spiritual leaders have people throwing opposition or accusation their way. Leaders aren't immune to the "Small Things Syndrome" either. They need courage to stand against condemnation and criticism. Be an encourager for your spiritual leaders. Boost their confidence through your prayers and specific biblical affirmation. Call or text them a biblical promise. Send an encouraging note. Post something positive about their leadership online. Do this today!

For God to call him servant, son, and signet ring was an affirmation of Z's identity and an acknowledgment of God's confidence in him. Granted, God didn't call Zerubbabel His son, but he did identify him as the son of Shealtiel. Remember from our study in Session One, this is an important designation because that made Zerubbabel a grandson of King Jehoiachin of Judah, thus a descendant of David, putting Z in the line of Jesus, the Son who was to come.

God identifies you in similar fashion. Let me show you how.

Turn to John 1:12 and Galatians 3:26. What do these verses say about your identity?

What do John 12:26 and 1 Peter 2:15-16 suggest about your role?

Now look at Luke 9:1; 10:19, and 2 Corinthians 5:18-20. What do these verses suggest about your calling?

For God to call you His daughter, for Him to choose you to serve Him, and for Him to give you the authority of His Son—as if you were His very own signet ring—shows your true identity in Christ and affirms God's confidence in you.

Understanding the truths in these verses as part of God's One-on-one message to you, how can they help you take courage? Journal below your thoughts on who you are in Christ and His purpose for you as stated in these passages.

Because I am God's child, I . . .

Because I am God's servant, I . . .

Because I have authority in Christ, I . . .

My friend, you are just as significant to God as Zerubbabel was. You are God's daughter, and His servant. You bear His authority, and so do I. That's why we can take courage to the very end!

Haggai 2:23 may be the end of the Book of Haggai, but it's not the end of the story. Zerubbabel was given a promise, and God keeps His promises. Although the prophecies surrounding Zerubbabel in this passage did not fully come to pass in his day, we can't overlook that he was just a representative of the greater Zerubbabel to come.[9] Generations after Zerubbabel died, his descendant was born in Bethlehem and dedicated in that very same temple that Haggai and the Jews were faithful to rebuild (Luke 2:22-38). Long after Zerubbabel closed his eyes to this world, God's ultimate Signet Ring came, and we beheld His glory, "the glory of the one and only Son, who came from the Father, full of grace and truth" (John 1:14, NIV).

Pause here and let that sink in. Rephrase Luke 1:74-75 into a prayer. Use as many words in the two verses as you can to praise the Lord, thank Him, and commit your whole heart and service to Him.

Dear Jesus,

Amen.

Haggai encouraged the people to build the temple, not just for their purpose and their day, but for what was to come—or rather for who was to come in the future. They weren't just building for the present; they were building for the promise.

You are, too. You must faithfully invest your life today in God's purposes, trusting Him for results you may never see.

Stay faithful, my friend. Consider your ways and prioritize your days. Do the next right thing and obey no matter what. Lean into God's presence and avoid the comparison trap. Do your one thing and live stirred up. Be patient with the seed and do not fear. The investments you make today are for the glory of God and the good of generations to come.

Your work matters just like the Jews' work mattered, even though their efforts were full of fits and starts, distraction and discouragement, fatigue and faithfulness.

No matter what you face or how you feel, take courage, sister, and work, for God is with you (Hag. 2:4).

Well, I guess we need to wrap this up. I will leave you with these final encouragements from my heart to yours . . .

When the landscape of your life seems dotted with the rubble of hopelessness, take courage, you are not alone. God is with you, and He will give you strength to rebuild what is broken.

On those days when your priorities get confused, take courage and consider your ways. God will stir your spirit to do the next right thing.

When you're worn out and feel like your fatigue is stronger than your faith, take courage. God will strengthen your hands and your heart.

During the times you feel like you can't stand up against accusation or opposition, take courage. Jesus will stand up tall in you and for you.

 Stay connected with me, please! I'm @JennRothschild on Twitter® and Instagram® and Jennifer Rothschild on Facebook. And we can hang out every week on my *4:13 Podcast* where I'll give you practical encouragement and biblical wisdom to live the "I Can" life!

In those barren seasons when you get weary in well-doing, and you can't see any success, take courage because you build more than you see.

When you're burdened by the weight of discouragement, take courage, my friend. A far greater weight of glory grounds and anchors you.

And, ultimately, when you feel like you just can't hold on to hope, take courage. You are held securely in the hand of God forever, just like a signet ring on His finger.

Oh, thank You, Lord, for courage. We love You with our whole hearts forever and always. Amen!

Girl, I'll miss hanging out with you and our guy Haggai! I'm cheering you on!

Bless you, my sweet sister,

Jennifer

May the God of endurance and encouragement grant you to live in such harmony with one another, in accord with Christ Jesus, that together you may with one voice glorify the God and Father of our Lord Jesus Christ.
ROMANS 15:5-6, ESV

Group session 1

Welcome and Prayer

VIDEO NOTES

The Four "I Cans" of Courageous Women

1. I can live _____.

The cost of __ _____ is far less than the price you pay when you live _____.

Living alert means to not be distracted and to live in _____.

2. I can stand _____ in the faith.

Courageous women go with what we _____—not with how we feel.

3. Be _____.

Be courageous in the original Greek, *andrizomai*, shows up one time in the New Testament and it literally means "_____ a _____."[1]

To be really courageous, we need to have an _____ perspective.

Endurance is _____ _____ in whatever "cross" God has allowed in your life.

In Hebrews 12:2 the word *despise* means "to consider it _____."[2]

To be courageous, to "be a man," do not allow your life to be governed by _____ but by faith.

4. I can be _____.

> Would you like to read my written summary of this video teaching? Just go to jenniferrothschild.com/takecourage

DAY 1: Do you ever try to use religious activity to mask your true spiritual condition? Explain.

How is sin contagious? How have you seen your sin lead others astray?

How do we remedy our separation from God caused by our sin?

DAY 2: What does it mean to have a "marker day," and what are some of yours? Why is it important that we have them?

What does it mean for God's mercy to be severe at times? What difficult experiences in your life have shown themselves to actually be God's grace and mercy at work?

DAY 3: Would you consider yourself to be a patient person? Why or why not? Why is patience such a needed attribute for your spiritual life?

Is there a spiritual "seed" you currently are waiting on to sprout and grow? Explain.

DAY 4: How does encouragement give us courage?

What's the difference between compliments and encouragement? Which do you think we need most? Why?

DAY 5: Why is finding your identity in Christ so important?

How would you define your identity in Christ?

To access the video teaching sessions, use the instructions in the back of your Bible study book.

BIBLE STUDY RESOURCES

There are so many resources available to help us dig deeper into God's Word. It's wonderful, but it can be overwhelming. Where to start? Who to trust? Here are a few tried and true go-to resources you can use during this study.

ONLINE TOOLS

- BibleGateway.com
- BibleHub.com
- BlueLetterBible.org
- BibleStudyTools.com
- The Bible App (YouVersion)
- Dwell Bible App (Visit JenniferRothschild.com/Dwell to see me use it and hear why it's one of my favorites.)

PRINT RESOURCES

The New Strong's Expanded Exhaustive Concordance of the Bible by James Strong
Matthew Henry's Concise Commentary on the Whole Bible
Holman Bible Commentaries
The New American Commentaries
The Zondervan Encyclopedia of the Bible by Merrill C. Tenney and Moisés Silva

LEADER HELPS

Thanks so much for leading your group through this study! I know you'll experience much joy and many blessings as you help walk your group through the study of Haggai. I'm praying for you as you take on this responsibility.

I've also put together a little something just for you, dear leader. Go to jenniferrothschild.com/takecourage to get it. Plus you'll find extra resources to enhance your study gatherings.

STUDY FORMAT

GROUP SESSIONS: Each group session contains the following elements: Welcome and Prayer / Watch the Video / Group Discussion. The group discussion provides questions generated from the previous week's personal study and the video teaching. Feel free to adapt, skip, or add questions according to the needs of your group.

PERSONAL STUDY: Each session contains five days of personal study to help participants dig into the Word of God for themselves.

BEING AN EFFECTIVE LEADER

Three keys to being an effective leader of your group:

1. PREPARE. Make sure you've watched the teaching video and completed each week's personal study before the group session. Review the discussion questions and consider how best to lead your group through this time.

2. PRAY. Set aside time each week to pray for yourself and for each member of your group. Though organizing and planning are important, protect your time of prayer before each gathering.

3. CONNECT. Find ways to interact and stay engaged with the women in your group throughout the study. Make use of social media, emails, and handwritten notes to encourage them. And don't stop the connection when the study ends. Continue to encourage and challenge the women in your group in their spiritual journey.

ENDNOTES

SESSION 1

1. *Encyclopedia Britannica*, s.v. "Confucius," accessed February 21, 2020, https://www.britannica.com/biography/Confucius.

2. *Encyclopedia Britannica*, s.v. "Pythagoras," accessed February 21, 2020, https://www.britannica.com/biography/Pythagoras.

3. Richard A. Taylor, *New American Commentary Vol 21A: Haggai, Malachi* (Nashville: B&H Publishing Group, 2004), accessed March 17, 2020, retrieved from https://app.wordsearchbible.com.

4. Charles R. Swindoll, "Haggai," *The Bible-Teaching Ministry of Charles R. Swindoll*, accessed March 30, 2020, https://www.insight.org/resources/bible/the-minor-prophets/haggai.

5. Taylor, *New American Commentary Vol 21A: Haggai, Malachi*.

6. Ibid.

7. Swindoll, "Haggai."

8. Taylor.

9. Charles Spurgeon, "Psalm 137," *A Treasury of David*, Spurgeon Archive, https://archive.spurgeon.org/treasury/ps137.php, accessed March 17, 2020.

10. Ibid.

11. Mervin Breneman. *New American Commentary Vol 10: Ezra, Nehemiah, Esther,* (Nashville: B&H Publishing Group, 2012), retrieved from https://app.wordsearchbible.lifeway.com.

12. J. A. Thompson, *New American Commentary Vol 09: 1, 2 Chronicles*, (Nashville: B&H Publishing Group, 1994), accessed January 11, 2020, retrieved from https://app.wordsearchbible.com.

13. Taylor.

SESSION 2

1. Richard A. Taylor, *New American Commentary Vol 21A: Haggai, Malachi* (Nashville: B&H Publishing Group, 2004), accessed January 14, 2020, retrieved from https://app.wordsearchbible.com.

2. Ibid.

3. Max Anders, ed. and Stephen Miller, *Holman Old Testament Commentary: Nahum–Malachi* (Nashville: Broadman & Holman Publishers, 2004), accessed January 14, 2020, retrieved from https://app.wordsearchbible.com.

4. Pieter A. Verhoef, *The New International Commentary on the Old Testament: the Books of Haggai and Malachi* (Grand Rapids, MI: William B. Eerdmans Publishing Co., 1987), 60.

5. Strong's H1870, *Blue Letter Bible,* accessed March 30, 2020, https://www.blueletterbible.org/lang/lexicon/lexicon.cfm?t=kjv&strongs=h1870.

6. "Definition of Muse," *Merriam-Webster*, accessed March 18, 2020, https://www.merriam-webster.com/dictionary/muse.

7. "Definition of a-," *Merriam-Webster*, accessed March 18, 2020, https://www.merriam-webster.com/dictionary/a-.

8. Craig Blomberg, *New American Commentary Vol 22: Matthew* (Nashville: B&H Publishing Group, 1992), accessed January 20, 2020, retrieved from https://app.wordsearchbible.com.

9. "Definition of heartily," *Merriam-Webster*, accessed January 20, 2020, https://www.merriam-webster.com/dictionary/heartily.

10. Taylor, *New American Commentary Vol 21A: Haggai, Malachi*.

11. Paul R. House, *New American Commentary Vol 08: 1, 2 Kings* (Nashville: B&H Publishing Group, 1995), accessed on March 18, 2020, retrieved from https://app.wordsearchbible.com.

SESSION 3

1. Richard A. Taylor, *The New American Commentary—Volume 21a, Haggai & Malachi* (Nashville: B&H Publishing Group, 2004), accessed January 23, 2020, retrieved from https://app.wordsearchbible.com.

2. Holman Reference Editorial Staff, "Cedar," *Holman Illustrated Bible Dictionary* Nashville: B&H Publishing Group, 2003), accessed January 23, 2020, retrieved from https://app.wordsearchbible.com.

3. Max Anders, ed. and Stephen Miller, *Holman Old Testament Commentary Nahum–Malachi* (Nashville: Broadman Holman, 2004), accessed January 23, 2020, retrieved from https://app.wordsearchbible.com.

4. John Piper, "God Is Most Glorified in Us When We Are Most Satisfied in Him," October, 13, 2012, accessed January 23, 2020, https://www.desiringgod.org/messages.

5. Elisabeth Elliot, *These Strange Ashes: Is God Still in Charge?* (Grand Rapids, MI: Revell, 1998), 147-148.

6. "Ezra 1:6." *Cambridge Bible for Schools and Colleges*, BibleHub.com, accessed February 11, 2020 , https://biblehub.com/commentaries/cambridge/ezra.

SESSION 4

1. "Definition of consecrated," *Dictionary.com*, accessed February 24, 2020, https://www.dictionary.com/browse/consecrated?s=t.

2. Richard A. Taylor, *New American Commentary Vol 21A: Haggai, Malachi* (Nashville: B&H Publishing Group, 2004), accessed March 18, 2020, retrieved from https://app.wordsearchbible.com.

3. "Definition of Work," *Dictionary.com*, accessed January 28, 2020, https://www.dictionary.com/browse/work.

4. Charles Spurgeon, "Psalm 27," *A Treasury of David*, Spurgeon Archive, accessed January 28, 2020, http://archive.spurgeon.org/treasury/ps027.php.

5. "Haggai 1:14," *BibleHub.com*, accessed March 18, 2020, https://biblehub.com/lexicon/haggai/1-14.htm.

6. Strong's G2041, *BibleHub.com*, accessed March 18, 2020, https://biblehub.com/greek/2041.htm.

7. Richard R. Melick, *New American Commentary Vol 32: Philippians, Colossians, Philemon* (Nashville: B&H Publishing Group, 1991), accessed January 28, 2020, retrieved from https://app.wordsearchbible.com.

8. Strong's G1756, *BibleHub*, accessed March 30, 2020, https://biblehub.com/greek/1756.htm.

9. "Haggai 2," *Cambridge Bible for Schools and Colleges*, accessed March 18, 2020, https://biblehub.com/commentaries/cambridge/haggai/2.htm.

10. Elisabeth Kübler-Ross and David Kessler, *Life Lessons: Two Experts on Death and Dying Teach Us About the Mysteries of Life and Living* (New York: Scriber, 2000), 138-139.

11. Brother Lawrence, *The Practice of the Presence of God* (Boston: New Seeds, 2013).

12. Brother Lawrence, as quoted by Richard J. Foster and James Bryan Smith, eds., *Devotional Classics: Selected Readings for Individuals and Groups* (San Francisco: HarperCollins, 1993.), 372.

13. Mareo McCracken, "The Only Thing You Need to Do to Overcome Fear, According to Neuroscience," *Inc.com,* accessed January 31, 2020, retrieved from https://inc.com.

SESSION 5

1. Strong's H2584, *Blue Letter Bible,* accessed March 30, 2020, https://www.blueletterbible.org/lang/lexicon/lexicon.cfm?t=kjv&strongs=h2584.

2. Richard A. Taylor, *New American Commentary Vol 21A: Haggai, Malachi* (Nashville: B&H Publishing Group, 2004), accessed March 18, 2020, retrieved from https://app.wordsearchbible.com.

3. "Haggai 2:6," *Cambridge Bible for Schools and Colleges*, accessed March 18, 2020, https://biblehub.com/commentaries/cambridge/haggai/2.htm.

4. "Hark! The Herald Angels Sing," *Timelesstruths.org*, accessed March 18, 2020, https://library.timelesstruths.org/music/Hark_the_Herald_Angels_Sing/.

5. "Who is the desired of all nations (Haggai 2:7)?", *GotQuestions*, accessed March 31, 2020, https://www.gotquestions.org/desired-of-all-nations.html.

6. Max Anders, ed. and Stephen Miller, *Holman Old Testament Commentary Nahum–Malachi* (Nashville: Broadman Holman, 2004), accessed March 19, 2020, retrieved from https://app.wordsearchbible.com.

7. Taylor, *New American Commentary Vol 21A: Haggai, Malachi.*

8. Ibid.

9. Anders, *Holman Old Testament Commentary Nahum–Malachi.*

10. C. S. Lewis, *The Weight of Glory and Other Addresses,* (Grand Rapids, MI: William B. Eerdmans Publishing Company, 1965), 4–5.

11. C. S. Lewis, *Mere Christianity,* (Samizdat, 2014), 75.

12. Steve Gregg, "Making Sense of Ezekiel's Temple Vision," *Christian Research Journal,* accessed March 19, 2020, retrieved from https://www.equip.org/article/making-sense-ezekiels-temple-vision.

13. Lamar Eugene Cooper Sr., *New American Commentary Vol 17: Ezekiel* (Nashville: B&H Publishing Group, 1994), accessed March 19, 2020, retrieved from https://app.wordsearchbible.com.

14. Strong's H7965, *Blue Letter Bible,* accessed March 30, 2020, https://www.blueletterbible.org/lang/lexicon/lexicon.cfm?t=kjv&strongs=h7965.

15. "Haggai 2:9," *BibleGateway.com,* accessed March 19, 2020, https://biblehub.com/lexicon/haggai/2-9.htm.

SESSION 6

1. *CSB Study Bible,* "Kaved" (Nashville, TN: Holman Bible Publishers, 2017), 1,076.

2. Strong's H1820, *Blue Letter Bible,* accessed February 24, 2020, https://www.blueletterbible.org/lang/lexicon/lexicon.cfm?t=kjv&strongs=h1820.

3. Andrew E. Hill, *Tyndale Commentaries* (Downers Grove, IL: InterVarsity Academic, 2015), 85, accessed February 10, 2020, retrieved from https://app.wordsearchbible.com.

4. Richard A. Taylor, *New American Commentary Vol 21A: Haggai, Malachi* (Nashville: B&H Publishing Group, 2004), accessed February 9, 2020, retrieved from https://app.wordsearchbible.com.

5. Strong's H3245, *Blue Letter Bible,* accessed March 30, 2020, https://www.blueletterbible.org/lang/lexicon/lexicon.cfm?t=kjv&strongs=h3245.

6. Taylor, *New American Commentary Vol 21A: Haggai, Malachi.*

7. Pieter A. Verhoef, *New International Commentary,* (Grand Rapids, MI: The Wm. B. Eerdmans Publishing Co., 1987), accessed February 10, 2020, retrieved from https://app.wordsearchbible.com.

8. "Encourage," *Online Etymology Dictionary,* accessed February 10, 2020, https://www.etymonline.com/word/encourage.

9. Taylor, *New American Commentary Vol 21A: Haggai, Malachi.*

SESSION 7

1. Strong's G407, *Blue Letter Bible,* accessed February 24, 2020, https://www.blueletterbible.org/lang/lexicon/lexicon.cfm?t=kjv&strongs=g407.

2. Strong's G2706, *Blue Letter Bible,* accessed March 30, 2020, blueletterbible.org/lang/lexicon/lexicon.cfm?t=kjv&strongs=g2706.

Notes

Notes

Additional Studies from
JENNIFER ROTHSCHILD

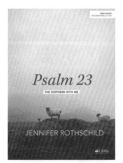

PSALM 23
7 Sessions

Explore the depths of God's compassionate care while gaining fresh insight and encouragement from Psalm 23.

lifeway.com/psalm23

HOSEA
7 Sessions

Dive into the passionate love story of Hosea to identify the modern-day idols in your life and step into the freedom of Christ.

lifeway.com/hosea

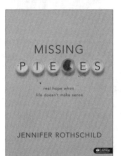

MISSING PIECES

7 Sessions

Explore the messy and mysterious uncertainties of faith to learn to trust Jesus over emotion.

lifeway.com/missingpieces

ME, MYSELF & LIES
7 Sessions

Examine your thoughts and words to identify the negativity in your daily inner dialogue and replace negative thoughts with positive truths from God's Word.

lifeway.com/memyselfandlies

lifeway.com/jenniferrothschild | 800.458.2772

Lifeway women

Bring FRESH GROUNDED FAITH *to* YOUR CHURCH

War Room's "Miss Clara"

LAURA **STORY**   LYSA **TERKEURST**   KAREN **ABERCROMBIE**   SHEILA **WALSH**

CANDACE CAMERON **BURE**   MEREDITH **ANDREWS**

FRESH GROUNDED FAITH

featuring

JENNIFER ROTHSCHILD
& SPECIAL GUESTS

***Local churches are the heartbeat of
Fresh Grounded Faith women's events.***

*In cities across America, we help a woman just like
you partner with a host church, and then bring area
churches together to connect women to God's Word
and each other. I'd love for my friends* and me to
bring some practical encouragement and Bible
teaching to the women you love ... so let's do
this together!*

Jennifer

* *Complete list of friends can be found
at FreshGroundedFaith.com.*

FRESHGROUNDEDFAITH.com

Get the most from your study.

IN THIS STUDY, YOU'LL:

• Defeat discouragement through God's presence, people, and Word.

• See beyond your current circumstances to a future hope.

• Learn to trust God more than your feelings.

STUDYING ON YOUR OWN?

Watch or listen to Jennifer Rothschild's teaching sessions, available for rent or purchase at lifeway.com/takecourage.

Browse companion products, a free session sample, video clips, church promotional materials, and more at

lifeway.com/takecourage